GHOST STORIES

of

MINNESOTA

Gina Teel

LONE
PINE

Lone Pine Publishing International

The Publisher: Lone Pine Publishing International
Distributed by Lone Pine Publishing
1808 B Street NW, Suite 140
Auburn, WA 98001
USA

Website: www.lonepinepublishing.com
        www.ghostbook.net

National Library of Canada Cataloguing in Publication Data
Teel, Gina, 1962–
    Ghost Stories of Minnesota
    ISBN-13: 978-1-894877-07-7
    ISBN-10: 1-894877-07-1

    1. Ghosts—Minnesota. 2. Legends—Minnesota. I. Title.
GR580.T43 2002   398.2'0977605   C2002-910280-4

Editorial Director: Nancy Foulds
Project Editors: Shelagh Kubish, Denise Dykstra
Illustrations Coordinator: Carol Woo
Production Coordinator: Jennifer Fafard
Book Design, Layout & Production: Lynett McKell
Cover Design: Gerry Dotto

Photo Credits: Every effort has been made to accurately credit photographers. Any errors or omissions should be directed to the publisher for changes in future editions. The photographs in this book are reproduced with the generous permission of their owners: Fitzgerald Theater, photo by Cheryl Walsh Bellville (p.63); Forepaugh's Restaurant, St. Paul (p.89); Hennepin History Museum, Minneapolis (p.72); Le Sueur County Historical Society Museum (p.81); Carol Lowell (p.171); Minnesota Historical Society, por/11918/p25 (p.128), MR2.9/FH3.2G/p16 (p.29), AV1988.45.153 (p.127), MR2.9/SP3.2q/p532 (p.43), FM6.143/r1 (p.123); Minnesota Historical Society, photo by Brimacombe, N7.4/p5 (p.54); Minnesota Historical Society, photo by C.J. Hibbard, MH5.9/MP8/p341 (p.137); Minnesota Historical Society, photo by A.F. Raymond, HD3.121/r6 (p.187); Saint Mary's University of Minnesota, Winona (p.113); Steve Tompkins, S&C Photography (p.145); Washington County Historical Museum (p.68).

The stories, folklore and legends in this book are based on the author's collection of sources including individuals whose experiences have led them to believe they have encountered phenomena of some kind or another. They are meant to enter- tain, and neither the publisher nor the author claims these stories represent fact.

PC: P6

To Jessica, for more than
one missed bedtime story

Contents

Acknowledgments 6
Introduction 8

Chapter 1: Haunted Houses
Gamble House Ghost 14
Spooked Students 20
The Unseen Guest 21
The Vanishing Cemetery 24
Boy Ghost 26
Willie Gibbs 29
For Pete's Sake 30
Houser House Ghost 32
A Never-ending Meeting Place 39
The Floating Face 39
Spectral Knocking 40
The Griggs Mansion 42
Flapjack Ghost 45
Swensson Farm 48

Chapter 2: Haunted Theaters & Museums
Long-term Usher 52
Christopher the Mischievous 55
Art Is Here 58
Ben and Veronica 63
Jokes by George 65
Ghostly Mother 67
Ambitious Apparitions 69
Mystery in the Museum 72
Area 35 74
Spooky Spectators 76
Invisible Apparition 80

Chapter 3: Spirits on the Menu
Benchwarmer Bob's 84
Saloon Spooks 85
Eatery Apparitions 87
Fine Dining Ghosts 88
Authorial Apparition? 92
A New Roommate 94

Chapter 4: Ghosts in Public

79 East Second Street 98
Wabasha Street Caves 101
Soldier Spirits 105
Revenge from the Hereafter 106
Haunting the State Fair 114
Looking for a Lost Lover 116
An Endless Execution 118
Uncanny Courthouse 119
State Capitol Specters 122
Riverview Hall Haunting 124
Loon Lake Cemetery 125
Ann Bilansky 127
A Mother's Revenge 129
Ghosts of a Government Center 130
A Vignette of Fright 131
The Hanging of John Moshik 134
Drowning Monk 138
Edelbrock Haunting 140
Ghost Bear 141
Phantom Photo 142

Chapter 5: Minnesota's Ghost Hunters

Send-off Psychic 154
Ghost Buster with a Gift 161
Deciphering Ghostly Clues 169
Investigating the Intangible 173
Footprints in the Snow 178

Chapter 6: Legends of Mysterious Minnesota

The Legend of the Blue Light 182
Witch Tree 183
New Year's Eve Ghost 184
Milford Mine 185
Moose Lake 188
The Ghost of Death 191
Fountain of Sorrow 192
Fox Farmer Phantom 193
Kitty Ging 194
Ghost Diver 197
The Strange Story of Annie Mary Twente 199
Ghostly Hitchhiker 205
Ghost Ship 206

Acknowledgments

This book wouldn't exist without the kindness and generosity of the many people who aided my research, provided leads on some great ghost stories and generally went out of their way to help me.

I'm equally indebted to those who bravely agreed to be interviewed about their experiences for this book despite the possibility of facing ridicule in their communities simply for admitting they believe in ghosts.

For their candor, bouquets to Rick Hagen of the Ghost Hunters Society of Minnesota, John Savage of the Minnesota Paranormal Investigative Group, Deborah Frethem of Down in History Tours Inc. and psychics Carol Lowell and Jean Kellett.

For their cooperation, kudos to fellow scribes John Brewer of the *Southwest Journal;* Don Boxmeyer at the *St. Paul Pioneer Press;* Laurel Parrott, editor at the *Camden Community News;* Jake Niemand, a.k.a. AJ Cooper, of KRAM 96 FM; Bill Morgan of the *St. Cloud Times;* and Donna Weber, news editor at *The Journal* in New Ulm.

For their informative responses to my queries, hats off to Jack Kabrud, curator of the Hennepin History Museum; Kris Howland, public relations director at the Chanhassen Dinner Theaters; Dennis Behl of the Guthrie Theater; Tom Grier of the Performing Arts Center at Winona State University; and Walter Lower, Jr., local historian at Moose Lake.

For treating my requests with respect, special thanks to Walter Bennick, archivist at the Winona County Historical Society; Brent Peterson, library manager at the Washington County Historical Society; Mona Nelson-Balcer, director of the Kandiyohi County Historical Society; Rosemarie Puerta Curnutt, archivist at the Stearns History Museum; the Le Sueur County Historical Society; Marilyn Anderson, editor of the Anoka County Genealogical Society; Ardyce Stein, director of the Roseau County Historical Society; June Lynne, director at the Chippewa County Historical Society; and Jeanne Anderson of the St. Louis Park Historical Society.

For sharing their fascinating—and sometimes terrifying—stories, a special mention to Tara and Bruce Forsyth; Mindy Schultz; Mark Hauser; Minnesota Assistant Attorney General J. P. Barone and his wife, Ramsey County Commissioner Victoria Reinhardt; Desmond Griffin; Pam Sicard; and Kimberly and Joseph Arrigoni. Finally, a special thank you to my sisters, Nancy and Chris, for persuading their friends to share their ghost stories with me, and to my mother, Joan, for making more than one trip to the library on my behalf.

Introduction

Growing up in the Twin Cities in the early 1970s, I often explored the area's historic homes and imagined how the rich barons and bootleggers who built them might have lived. It seemed only natural, then, to find myself some 30 years later writing a book about many of these same people and places. And it was no coincidence that I was writing about their ghosts.

My own encounter with the paranormal began in 1999, when I moved into a hacienda overlooking the North Saskatchewan River valley in Edmonton, Alberta, Canada.

The house was old, so I didn't read much into it when the lights flickered on and off, the comfortable room temperature suddenly dropped to freezing or blasts of cold air bombed through the house, making the hair on the back of my neck stand up.

But all that changed late one night as I headed to the basement. I opened the basement door and stopped dead in my tracks. A small piece of white paper, folded neatly in half, was suspended in the middle of the wall directly above the stairs.

I stared at it a moment, wondering how a piece of paper could have possibly come to rest in such an unlikely spot, before reaching up to take it down. I recognized the paper as soon as I opened it; it was a grading report from a creative writing course I'd taken at college back in 1988. Up until this point, it had been sealed away in a box in a corner of the basement with all my other college writing efforts.

Though the paper's appearance was certainly strange, I took comfort in rereading the encouraging message penned by my instructor more than a decade before, and not just because she'd given me an A– on the poetry assignment. I put the experience down to coincidence.

A week later, I headed down to the basement. This time I found an unframed print I own resting sideways on the same spot on the wall where I'd found the grading slip. The print features a young, brown-haired girl in a Victorian-era party dress looking at an Alice in Wonderland–type white rabbit. The last time I recalled seeing this print, it was upstairs under a pile of papers in a kitchen junk drawer.

This time I was not so dismissive. Recently my young, brown-haired daughter had been waking in the night frightened, saying someone was pinching her toes and pulling her fingertips. I had dismissed her complaints as a combination of bad dreams and a vivid imagination, but now I wasn't so sure.

I called my sister to see if she had placed the print there when she was baby-sitting the previous weekend. She assured me that she hadn't been anywhere near the basement.

I became more uncomfortable a day later when, searching for some sort of meaning, I turned the picture over to discover the name of the print house was "Portal."

A few evenings later, I discovered the comforter turned down on the side of my bed that I don't usually sleep on. What disturbed me about this particular encounter was that just a week or so earlier, I had twice awakened with a start on this same side of the bed with the distinct impression that I couldn't breathe because someone was pressing down on my lungs.

I broached the subject with a trusted friend, who then contacted a psychic. Over the phone the psychic told me she felt the presence was female and that it meant no harm. The psychic also sensed it was either my "Guide," which I interpreted to mean my guardian angel, or a wayward spirit that thought I could help it pass on to the other side. Then she offered to come over to my house to determine which it was.

As a journalist, I was curious to see the psychic in action. But I wanted more facts about the possible haunting first.

I tracked down former tenants of the rental property who still resided in Edmonton. One woman, a psychologist, sucked in her breath when I asked if she had had any unusual experiences in the house. "You just sent a shiver down my spine," she said and turned quite pale as she related her story.

In hushed tones she explained how she and her husband had endured unexplained loud crashing and scraping noises and seen bedroom doors open and close by themselves. She recalled the phenomena occurring in only two of the three bedrooms, the rooms my daughter and I used. She reported that the middle bedroom, my daughter's room, was the most active, and that her cat had spent hours playing there, batting its paws in thin air as if it were playing with some phantom toy.

The psychologist said other than being noisy, the spirit was largely benign. She added that she and her husband suspected the spirit belonged to a woman named Elizabeth, who had lived in the home years earlier. According to neighbors, Elizabeth had been quite attached to the property and its rambling, old-style rose, lilac and herb gardens—so much so that even after falling victim to a degenerative brain disease and being moved to an extended care facility, Elizabeth would regularly turn up at her beloved home in a disoriented state. Apparently this behavior continued until she died.

I called the property manager to verify the information on Elizabeth, only to discover a second possible explanation for the phenomena.

It turned out that a young woman named Lois had died in the house when seven months pregnant. The story goes that Lois, a doctor's wife, had been reading a bedtime story to their young son. After a while, her husband called out to her but got no response. He found her collapsed on the floor, dead from a brain aneurysm.

The young doctor remained in the house with their son. He later remarried, and his new wife and their combined family lived happily in the house for a year before moving away. This fact I was able to substantiate: the family were indeed the last tenants in the home prior to my taking it over. Another eerie coincidence is that I had met the family during two pre-lease tours of the property, one of which occurred on the eve of the doctor's wedding to his new bride.

Psychics I interviewed for this book say that hauntings are a ghost's way of getting our attention. Lois, Elizabeth, or whoever was haunting that house, certainly got my attention, as did another ghost recently, albeit in a roundabout way.

I was talking recently with Rick Hagen, founder of the Ghost Hunters Society of Minnesota, about his investigation of a haunted mansion on Summit Avenue in St. Paul. I'd been invited to search this same house for ghosts on my next visit to the Twin Cities and was looking forward to it. Until I talked to Rick, that is.

While in the basement of the house, Rick became so overwhelmed by a feeling of oppression that he had to leave the wine cellar area and walk back out into the main basement. As he stood there trying to regain his composure, another psychic approached him and asked him if he was Rick.

Rick nodded. The psychic said he was getting a message for him from the other side, from "Alg, Al, Al Olson, it's Al Olson." Alger Olson, or Al, was the co-founder of the Ghost Hunters Society of Minnesota and a decade-long friend of Rick's. He died in 2001.

Rick told the psychic that he knew Al Olson.

The psychic relayed Al's urgent message: "Al says to get out of there as fast as you can right now because it's really bad stuff."

Rick heeded Al's message and immediately left the basement. Come to think of it, I'll probably heed Al's advice too and stay out of the basement when I'm there. After all, I've learned that it's important to pay attention to messages from the other side when they come your way, no matter how they're delivered.

1
Haunted
Houses

~

The thought of living in a haunted house, with some paranormal presence lurking in the darkest corners of the basement, terrifies most people. But not all hauntings are created equal.

Some spirits never interact directly with the living but simply carry on with routines they had in life. Those that met with a sudden and violent end often leave behind a powerful emotional imprint of their final moments, an unsettling sensation easily detected, but not always understood, by the living. Mischievous spirits play with the lights and electrical appliances and move objects to get themselves noticed.

Finally, there are spirits that have much more evil intentions in mind. These spirits tend to use aggression to drive a person from a house.

Most of the ghosts whose stories are recounted in this chapter had more sociable intentions in mind. But be forewarned—I did say most, not all.

~

Gamble House Ghost

James Gamble was a wealthy lumber merchant with exacting tastes and a need for things to be just so. In 1883 he commissioned architect George Wirth to design his dream home and spared no expense in building the imposing three-story Queen Anne sandstone mansion on St. Paul's famous Summit Avenue.

Gamble sold the house to the E.L. Hersey family in the early 1900s, and by 1930 the interior of the sprawling estate had been carved into four apartments. But some tenants at 475 Summit are convinced that Gamble never left the building, for he is still making his preferences known, even if it is from beyond the grave.

Mindy Schultz, who moved into a main-floor residence in the building in the spring of 2001, says furniture in some of the apartments is sometimes mysteriously rearranged. She believes "James…wants the house in its original state, so he moves things around as he'd like to see them."

Schultz says she's spent several nights in her Jeep in the driveway because she's been too frightened to sleep in the house. She's positive the place is haunted. "I live in a part of the house that would have been the main kitchen area, and I think that a maid or a servant from the Gamble home still haunts this area," she says. "I find my kitchen cupboard doors open…and it's not just one, it's usually all of them. And they are the old type that actually latch, so it is not as if the wind just blew them open."

This activity occurs up to six times a day, Schultz says. And often it is accompanied by footsteps. Schultz has also heard children's voices and laughter in her apartment late at night. And she claims there is a ghost around that likes to play with her Basset Hound, having the dog perform rollovers for hours on end.

There is the usual battery of electrical phenomena in the house, too: televisions turning on and off by themselves, the volume on radios suddenly cranking up, top-40 radio stations switching to classical music stations, CD players coming on, lights switching on and off. And in one bedroom that was originally a child's playroom, locked windows refuse to stay shut.

Despite the hauntings, Schultz says she's never noticed any unusual cold spots in the house, "mostly because the house itself is just plain cold." She has felt the odd draft in the bathroom, though. "If I'm in the shower sometimes with the door closed [there are no other windows or vents] the shower curtain will strangely kind of blow in as if a draft came from somewhere," she says. "The air is ice cold. I still blame that one on the maid looking for her kitchen. Who knows? But I can tell you that draft shouldn't be coming from anywhere."

John Savage, founder of the Minnesota Paranormal Investigative Group, first examined the house in 2000. He concluded it was haunted by at least two dozen ghosts. The ringleader, he says, is the ghost of James Gamble, who spooks the home from a closet in a back bedroom on the second floor. "[Gamble] is the father figure of the house and [he] has a deep attachment to Katie," says Savage, referring to Katie Nelson, who has lived on the building's second floor for two years.

According to Savage, the ghost of James Gamble calls Nelson "Kitty Cat" and is fond of her because she reminds him of his wife. Nelson has noticed this fondness. "He follows me around a lot," she says. "Apparently I have the same kind of lively personality and spirit as his wife."

Nelson realized there was something strange in the building the weekend after she moved in. "I kept hearing someone walking directly behind me. I kept turning around to see who it was and no one was there," she says. "Other times when I was up in my bedroom and alone in the house, I could hear someone open and close the downstairs door and [walk] up the steps. I'd call out but no one was ever there."

The spirit of James Gamble may be devotedly attached to Nelson, but he's also created tension between her and some of the other tenants in the building. She recalls an incident in which a former renter on the main floor accused her of dragging furniture, throwing heavy items and stomping loudly on a nightly basis, usually around 3 AM.

Nelson assured her neighbor that she and her roommates were usually in bed by 11 PM and therefore could not be responsible for the noise. She maintained that the sounds must have been coming from somewhere else in the house. The woman seemed satisfied with this explanation until the next night, when she knocked on Nelson's door.

"She was upset because the noise had started again and she thought it was us," Nelson says. Of course, the woman became concerned when she saw that there was no one in the apartment but Nelson, and that Nelson was talking to her, not throwing furniture around. Nelson accompanied the woman downstairs to her main-floor apartment, and sure enough she could hear the racket.

According to Savage, the tenants were detecting the restless ghost of James Gamble, who was expressing his frustration at not having things "just so" in his home. "John said the ghost was upset because his chair wasn't in the right spot and he couldn't find his liquor cart," Nelson explains. "He was wondering where the gas fixtures were and he didn't like the color of the living room, which he said was supposed to be burgundy."

While the ghost of James Gamble can be helpful—he turns lights on and off for her—Nelson says he can also be a real pain. She describes him as a near-obsessive neat freak who hounds her as she cleans, letting her know when the job she's done is not quite adequate. "I can literally feel him breathing down my neck," Nelson says. "He doesn't like the way I mop. We have claw-foot bathtubs and I only mop under them so far. He doesn't like that."

Nelson says her encounters with the ghost occur so often that she now communicates with him psychically and via a dowsing rod fashioned out of a wire coat hanger. (The hanger, shaped as an *L*, picks up vibrations from the ghost and points in the ghost's direction.) However, she's not always sure when he's around.

"He knows he's dead but he actually chooses to come back here," Nelson explains. "He's not here all the time but this is home for him and he makes sure the house is okay. From what I gather he pretty much comes back over because he's taking care of the house."

When he wants to, the ghost of James Gamble is good at getting Nelson's attention. On one occasion, while she was on the phone with Savage, he pushed her Dalmatian, Daisy, sideways on her hindquarters. On other occasions he's made his presence known by wildly swinging the chain lock on her bedroom door and the chain pull on her bedside table lamp. And sometimes he's flicked the lights on and off until she's acknowledged his presence.

But Gamble is not the only ghost Nelson has noticed. She's also heard the spirit of a little boy named Willie laughing and running around the house. Willie is somewhere between 8 and 12 years old. One tenant claims he constantly plays with toys she has stored away in a box for her grandchildren when they come to visit.

"She [the tenant] would come home from work and find the toys all over the living room floor," Nelson explains. "She'd put the toys away but the next day when she came home the toys would be all over the place again."

Another ghost inhabits a main-floor bedroom that was the home's original smoking lounge. Nelson says people sleeping in this bedroom wake up to the bed shaking and the distinct sensation that someone is crawling on top of them. "They try to get up because the bed is shaking and then they are pinned down by some unseen force," she says.

Savage has been through the house many times. On a recent sweep, he was able to capture three orbs on video. The orbs zipped around the frame and one actually disappeared into a pillar. The ghost of James Gamble claimed responsibility. "We told him we wanted to see him. He said he was all three orbs, which were captured at different times," Nelson says. "It's really quite neat; if you slow it down frame by frame you can see the shapes morphing as they move."

Savage says one of the strangest incidents that occurred in the house happened in one of the apartments' bedrooms. "One night during the investigation we walked into one of the bedrooms to find a bunch of pennies on the floor forming a perfect circle around the bed," he explains. "The person that slept in that room hadn't even been home for three days and later said they knew nothing about the pennies."

Savage was able to confirm that the ghost in Schultz's ground-floor apartment is that of a former servant. And he says that ghost is occasionally joined by a few others who come up from the basement. "Beside the cellar room is a pool room that, in my opinion, is set up like an old speakeasy," Savage says, "which, of course, was [a common thing] during the days of Prohibition in St. Paul."

Savage believes this is the area where the majority of the home's ghosts reside. "There are several entities down there in the cellar that I wouldn't want in my house," he says. "The majority of them are down in the pool room. When you walk in, you get the feeling that everyone is looking at you and there is a great sense of unease."

Savage calls this sense of unease a "residual haunting." He describes it as an emotional imprint that is left to linger in a certain area, in this case the pool room/speakeasy.

Savage believes there are sinister entities in the cellar. Yet Nelson has no plans to move out of the building any time soon. She's quite comfortable sharing the house with ghosts, provided they stay within their boundaries. Her reasons have more to do with nostalgia than cheap rent.

"I'm a fan of F. Scott Fitzgerald. He wrote about this house in *This Side of Paradise*, his first published novel," Nelson says. "Also, he was dating a woman who was staying in this house with a relative. He got his first kiss in my living room right in front of the fireplace."

Indeed, according to *St. Paul's Historic Summit Avenue*, Fitzgerald lived down the street while revising the manuscript of *This Side of Paradise* in 1919. And when his publisher accepted the novel, he is said to have danced down Summit Avenue, stopping friends and strangers to tell them the good news.

Spooked Students

The house at 362 Cummings Street in Winona is said to be haunted by a ghost with a flair for the dramatic. Besides following people around, this spirit likes to make his presence known by opening dead-bolted doors, moving objects, and making loud crashing noises that reportedly sound—strangely enough—like someone breaking fine china.

And though these cues are hard for any among the living to miss, the ghost occasionally feels the need to make his presence known in other ways as well. Over the years renters in the house have reported strange noises coming from the furnace room in the basement, as if someone in a great rage was pounding his or her fists on the furnace ducts.

Two students of Winona State University who lived in the house heard the sound and, to this day, they claim the house is haunted. Both tenants experienced a number of frightening incidents that left them badly shaken.

Tired of dorm life, the friends moved to the house on Cummings Street in their second year of university. They shared the spacious older home with three other students. Though the house was slightly run-down and in need of a few repairs, the renters were pleased with their new surroundings.

Things took a dramatic turn for the worse one October, just before Halloween. One of the students went to bed but found the bedroom so cold that it was impossible for him to fall asleep. He got up to get another blanket from the closet and froze in his tracks, and not because of the bone-chilling temperature in his room.

His fright was caused by the shadowy outline of a human figure on the wall near the closet door. Thinking it was his friends playing a trick on him, the student turned around. He fully expected to find one of his roommates standing there. But no one was there. The student panicked and reached for the light switch. As he flipped on the lights, the shadow appeared to duck into the closet.

Later that evening, a second tenant in a bedroom in another part of the house also saw a dark shadowy human figure outlined on a wall.

Several weeks later, the students were gathered in the living room watching late-night television when one of them happened to glance at the window. In the window, directly behind his reflection, stood a large dark human shape. When the student turned around, however, no one was there.

The strange and unexplained phenomena escalated from there, with many odd events happening in the kitchen area of the house near where the basement door—always locked with a dead-bolt—was located.

The occurrences came to a head one evening during a party, when the knocking on the furnace began. The pounding grew louder and louder, causing the students to flee the living room and run through the kitchen in a scramble to get out the back door. They stopped, dumbfounded, at the sight of the basement door flung wide open, the dead-bolt unfastened by what they could only imagine were ghostly hands.

The Unseen Guest

Many people dream about living in a rustic cabin nestled deep in the forest. But for retired trapper Rudy Billberg of Roseau County, life in a rustic cabin turned out to be a veritable nightmare.

Rudy was a young man when he moved into his logging cabin in the Big Woods. He was fresh out of high school when he experienced the first of many ghostly encounters he would endure in the tiny cabin. Ardyce Stein, director of the Roseau County Historical Society, provided this story.

In the winter of 1933 jobs were scarce, so Rudy and his friend Ed decided to make a living trapping and harvesting fur. They found a log shack in the Big Woods that was usable and, after some cleaning and repairing, moved in. "Our hearts sang as we planned our winter," Rudy says. "I would lay out my line to the east and Ed would go west...It was going to be a great adventure."

On November 1—the opening of the trapping season—the two began to work. For about three weeks their lives as trappers went as they expected. Their fur harvest was modest but they were satisfied. Then one evening everything changed.

"The weather was nice. The wind was calm. We had about six to eight inches of snow on the ground," Rudy remembers. "It was Sunday and this was the day we stayed home to rest and do the necessary baking and cleaning. That evening we sat reading magazines, I, stories of the Wild West, and Ed, a *True Detective* magazine. All at once I sat up straight. 'Listen, Ed, somebody's coming,' I said."

Rudy had heard footsteps moving from the soft snow to the packed area in front of their door. Other than he and Ed, only two old bachelors lived in the area, and he thought the footsteps were made by one of them. But when he got up and opened the door, he realized he was wrong.

"I opened the door. There was no one there!" he says. "We grabbed our flashlights and rushed outside. There was no sign of anyone. [Yet] no one could have moved away fast enough to get out of sight. We would have seen and heard him."

Rudy and Ed talked late into the night but could not come up with an explanation for the strange event. Eventually they decided to get some sleep and check for tracks in the morning. At the first sign of light they went outside. They searched the ground but found nothing. So they tried to forget the incident.

A week later the pair heard the footsteps again. And a couple of days after that, they heard them again. The nocturnal visits continued—sometimes a day apart, sometimes seven days. Yet each time there was no knock on the door. And each time there was nobody to be seen.

"On one occasion I sat by the table facing the window. It was a dark night and my kerosene lamp wasn't bright enough to cast any light beyond the window," Rudy says. "This time [the visitor] came to the door, then turned to walk all the way around the cabin. My eyes were about two feet from the glass and they grew to about the size of golf balls as his footsteps approached the window. Nobody passed by but we could hear him."

That did it. The two stayed home all the next day and inspected every inch of the cabin. They checked every log, the stovepipe, the cellar and the roof. They eliminated every possible cause of the clatter. They were stumped.

Time went on. "The visitor would come and Ed would say, 'Here comes our friend again.'" Rudy says. Then one night, after it had just stopped snowing, the two came up with a plan. "When he comes again,' Ed said, 'We'll wait till he comes to the door, then we will rush out. You go right and I'll go left; we'll meet in the back.' We did this and found nothing but each other."

Rudy and Ed left the woods in mid-February. They told their story to a local historian. He listened attentively and said he would do some checking. A couple of days later he informed the pair that he had learned of a man who had been seriously injured at the lumber camp. The man was taken to town on a bobsled, but died almost as soon as he got there. "Could his spirit have returned to the Big Woods?" Rudy asks.

Years later, on a visit to his hometown, Rudy returned to the Big Woods to see if his ghostly friend was still there. "I found nothing. All the old shacks had long since burned to the ground," he says. "I sadly walked away from the ashes. My mind was filled with memories of the winter when Ed and I lived there. What on earth was going on? We will never know."

The Vanishing Cemetery

The life span of the Mount Pleasant Cemetery in Columbia Heights, Anoka County, was brief, but the spirits that haunt the grounds have lasted much longer.

Houses now stand on the 10-acre parcel of land where headstones once stood. But eerie, unexplained events have area residents mighty suspicious that not quite all of the remains interred at Mount Pleasant Cemetery were trans-ferred to the new cemetery before the houses were built.

One of the biggest clues that things were amiss was when something strange happened just after the new dwellings went up, says Marilyn Anderson of the Anoka County Genealogical Society. According to sources at the local library, as new homeowners started to landscape and put in gardens, headstones would surface in the yards. "Residents of the area have stated many times that the area felt haunted," says Anderson.

The cemetery opened in 1901 as the Horace Lowry Cemetery. It was named after the son of local developer Thomas Lowry. Through his agency with the Twin City Lines, Thomas had promoted the sale of Columbia Heights property, built a hotel and established the cemetery, so it made perfect sense to stamp the family name on part of his legacy.

On opening day, the 10-acre parcel of prime real estate in the city's northeast was dedicated to the "public forever" by its namesake, Horace Lowry, and his wife, Kate. Later, however, Horace—perhaps no longer happy with his association in life with the dead—had his name removed, and the cemetery was renamed the Mount Pleasant Cemetery.

The cemetery was abandoned in 1915 and sat until December 6, 1937, when the city council of Columbia Heights deeded the land to the Columbia Investment Company of South Dakota for a new housing development called Oak Park. Working with the Walton Real Estate Company, the Columbia Investment Company divided the abandoned area of the Mount Pleasant cemetery into lots.

It has been stated that the Columbia Investment Company believed that "most" of the remains interred there were transferred to another cemetery. However, Anderson says, "The only records listing the names of those interred or where the bodies were transferred were held by the real estate company, which has been out of business for many years. We have no way of finding out the information."

Anderson does note that a local resident recently mentioned that he thought some of the remains were transferred to the cemetery off 5th Street and 53rd Avenue in Fridley, and then transferred again to the cemetery off Old Central.

Boy Ghost

Haunting a house along a quiet tree-lined residential street in Winona is the ghost of a young boy believed to have died more than 100 years ago, long before the area was ever platted for housing.

The boy was killed in a freak accident in the early 1900s: a team of horses that was pulling the wagon he rode in became spooked by some unseen force and bolted at full gallop down a steep hill, tipping the wagon over in the process and tossing the boy onto the hard ground with deadly force.

It is said the boy's spirit never left the spot where he met his death. Unfortunately, today there happens to be a home standing on that spot. And to make matters worse, the majority of the ghostly encounters occur in the bathroom—whether it is occupied or not.

The ghost first made himself known to the family about six months after they'd moved into their new custom-built home. The family was in the middle of dinner preparations when the air in the kitchen suddenly turned icy cold and an eerie silence fell over the room, leaving the children momentarily unable to hear the conversation they had seconds earlier been happily engaged in.

Suddenly the family heard what sounded like a boy yelling for his mother. The shouts were coming from the garage, but when the startled group investigated they found no one there. From then on it was not unusual to hear the sound of footsteps in empty hallways or on the staircase. The family's dogs became nervous and began acting strangely, whining at times as if they were looking at something that scared them. From the main floor of the house, a noise was often heard that sounded like furniture being dragged around in an upstairs bedroom. Again, however, no one was found when someone went up to investigate. The incidents escalated until the ghost finally showed himself to one of the children.

The child woke up in the middle of the night needing to go to the bathroom. She left her bedroom and walked down the hallway. As she neared the bathroom, she noticed that the light was on but the door was closed. Suddenly the door opened and the luminous figure of a young boy with blond hair walked out of the bathroom and right by the sleepy girl without so much as a word or a glance. Then he disappeared into her brother's bedroom.

Confused by the sight of a strange glowing boy in her house, especially one very similar in appearance to her older brother, the girl followed his footsteps down the hall to her brother's bedroom and opened the door. But the ghost boy was not there. Neither was her brother. Frightened, she ran to her mother's room and opened the door. There she found her brother fast asleep on the floor beside their mother's bed. Again there was no sign of the boy ghost anywhere.

The young girl was so upset by the encounter that she began keeping her bedroom door shut tight at night.

After a while the family determined that the ghost of the mysterious blond boy appeared most often in the bathroom, usually manifesting at the back outside wall and then walking across the floor to the door. Here he paused briefly, sometimes glancing at whoever happened to be in the bathroom—no matter what they happened to be doing—before walking through the door and down the hall to the brother's bedroom, where he promptly disappeared.

Just such an encounter occurred one night when the girl awoke suddenly to the sound of her bedroom door being thrown open. Standing in the doorway watching her was the ghost boy, his eerie white light easily visible against the darkness of the hallway. He stared a moment at the girl—who was paralyzed with fear—then went down the hallway in the direction of her brother's bedroom and disappeared.

The bathroom was the scene of the next encounter the girl had with the boy ghost. This time he spoke to her rather than reveal himself. The youngster had stepped out of the shower and was toweling off when she heard a male voice say, "You'd better get your clothes on." The startled girl wrapped the towel around herself and looked around, but she was completely alone.

The family contacted a ghost buster, who helped them accept that they were sharing their home with a ghost. To this day, they haven't quite figured out what the ghost wants, but they do believe he has some sort of message he wants to impart.

The family strongly believes that the ghost is actively seeking out the children, but not to purposely frighten them. They simply believe the children are more sensitive to the ghost, especially because the ghost himself is that of a child. The other connection may have to do with the son whom the ghost boy resembles. Could it be that a ghost from the past is haunting his own future to make sure the same tragic mistake doesn't repeat itself?

Until the family is successful in deciphering the boy ghost's message, his reason for being there is anyone's guess.

Willie Gibbs

Thousands of tourists visit the historic Gibbs Museum in St. Paul each year hoping to catch a glimpse of life in late 19th-century Minnesota, and some of them have seen the ghost of little Willie Gibbs, who became an unwilling victim of that life.

Willie died at the age of nine after fighting a prairie fire with his father, mother and older brother in a last-ditch effort to save the family homestead and the big new farmhouse his father was having built nearby. The houses were saved but Willie succumbed to the smoke. He never set foot inside his family's proud new home. It seems only fitting that Willie should inhabit the Gibbs house in death since he was cheated of the chance in life.

Over the years, dozens of people have reported seeing the ghostly lad at the farm, with perhaps the most reliable sighting occurring in 1996. At that time a deputy with the Ramsey

Young Willie Gibbs is said to haunt his family's farmhouse, which he never got a chance to live in before he died.

County Sheriff's Department was patrolling the site. He looked up into a window and saw a child's face looking down at him.

Other people have reported seeing a rocking chair rocking by itself. But the strangest things are reserved for the bedroom that was to have been Willie's. Witnesses claim that if you call Willie's name in the bedroom, the door to his wardrobe will open and close.

Site manager Ted Lau doesn't believe in ghosts but admits he's had a similar experience. "Occasionally we get a cupboard door or closet door opening for no reason," he says. "It happened to me. I was standing in the doorway to the bedroom talking to some people and the closet door opened for no reason. Of course, Willie Gibbs died in a fire here, so everyone thinks it was him. But I think it's because the floors are uneven, so you can step in one place and make something happen in another area of the house."

Maybe so. But that doesn't explain the impression of a child's body in Willie's bed that never goes away no matter how many times the mattress and covers are fluffed.

For Pete's Sake

When the Marthaler family purchased the old Thurmes homestead in Dakota County back in 1966, the nearest living soul was a neighbor well over a mile and a quarter away. Or so they thought.

Shortly after moving into the farmhouse, it became evident the family was sharing the 100-acre spread with a ghost. Lights would turn on and off by themselves, the crystals on the kitchen chandelier would suddenly shake and pictures on the walls would mysteriously fall off their hooks.

But Gail Marthaler says the ghost she calls Pete was most active outside. For years the family heard sounds of a vehicle driving up the gravel road towards the house and of a person walking in the yard. Try as they might, they never did see a car or an individual that could account for these sounds.

One time the horn in an old automobile parked on the property went off and wouldn't stop blaring. Marthaler's husband had to cut the wires to turn it off. Other times family members would head to the barn to do chores, only to find a fan turned on or the lights blazing.

Despite these regular goings-on, Marthaler says her family did not fear the ghost. "Nobody was ever afraid of him; we just existed beside him," she says. "And nobody ever saw him, but we always knew he was there. You could always hear him."

Marthaler believes the ghost is that of the homestead's original owner, Pete Thurmes. According to relatives, Pete, an old bachelor, fancied himself a mechanic and used to spend hours tinkering and repairing vehicles out in the yard. In 1955 he met a most mysterious death, sparking a whodunit debate that hasn't yet been laid to rest.

Pete was found dead in the woods across the road from his place, apparently from a shotgun blast. What was strange was the way his body was discovered: his hat was pulled over his head and his belt was wound around his neck. A pair of thick, clumsy mittens were on his hands.

His death was officially ruled a suicide, but Pete's relatives disputed the finding, noting the strange positioning of his hat and belt and that the thick mittens on his hands would have prevented him from pulling the trigger. They were convinced the old bachelor had been murdered—for money—and they even had a suspect: Pete's former stepson.

Pete had been married to a woman named Mabel Anderson, who had a son from a previous relationship. Pete had a habit of burying all his money under a tree in the woods, and the story goes that Mabel's son killed him for it.

The death was written up in *Life* magazine as one of the year's unsolved mysteries.

Marthaler says that Pete hasn't been around as much in the last five years, since the house was totally renovated. Perhaps it was simply time for him to move on. In 2000, the Thurmes farm was declared a century farm by Dakota County.

Houser House Ghost

Most realtors distribute pens and calendars as a way of saying thanks. But Minneapolis-based realtor Susan Lichliter ventures into the great beyond by offering potential buyers ghost-busting services for their new homes.

Lichliter began offering the service in 1996 when one of her clients, Mark Houser, called her to ask if she had known the handsome 1920s Mediterranean-style mansion he bought was haunted.

"I didn't [know it was haunted], but my mind immediately went back to a weird incident I had on the third floor of that house before Mark owned it," Lichliter says. "It was a huge, open, wonderful attic that was turned into a family room. When I was up there, there was a big 'whoosh' that went right past me. It wasn't cold—but it was different—and then it pushed me. I didn't know what it was and I didn't say anything. I just quickly went downstairs and outside."

Lichliter was unaware that she had just been attacked by a malicious ghost that would eventually put Houser and his teenage children through two years of hell.

Houser bought the house after his divorce. He chose it because it was a homey place where his two kids could stay on weekends, and because it was the "ultimate bachelor pad." He'd barely moved his belongings in when the trouble began. "I walked into a room that used to be a cellar and I remember feeling like I was being electrocuted. It was quite a jolt," he says. "I remember walking out of there thinking what…was that?"

Soon after, Houser's children came for a weekend stay. His daughter's visit was cut short, however. "That evening, my daughter started crying and screaming that she didn't like the house and she wanted to go home," Houser says. He tried to get her to explain but she wouldn't, so he took her home.

A few days later, Houser arrived home from work to find the sound of children's voices coming from the third floor. He thought it was his kids, who were supposed to be at their mom's. He called upstairs. The voices stopped. He got no answer.

Then Houser realized that the voices he had heard were from children far younger than his own. "My kids are teenagers and those were the voices of four- and five-year-olds," he says. "They were also speaking in a language I didn't recognize."

Houser climbed the stairs to the third floor. The voices started again as he made his way up. But the room was empty when he reached the top of the stairs, leaving the staunch nonbeliever in ghosts concerned that the stress of his divorce may have taken its toll on his mental health.

Shortly after that, Houser's son, Andy, told him the house had ghosts. "Andy told me there were five ghosts upstairs that had come from an orphanage that used to be about four blocks away but was destroyed in a fire," Houser says. "The children had died in the fire. The reason they went to the third floor is that they wanted to have a nice area to play in. I asked Andy how he knew this and he told me that he could see the ghosts and that he talked to them all the time. I told him I had heard them, too. When I asked Andy how he could possibly understand what they were saying, he looked at me oddly and said, 'Dad, they speak English.' "

As upset as Houser was, he was relieved to know he wasn't losing his mind. Relief quickly turned to anger, however, when Andy disclosed that another ghost in the house—Roger—had repeatedly tried to sexually molest him and his sister, Erin. Andy said the ghost had pinned him on his bed. It had abused Erin the same way.

Houser snapped when he learned his children were under attack. Suddenly he understood Erin's refusal to stay at his house. He called a business associate to get the name of a ghost buster the associate had hired to rid his home of a ghost. The thought of his children being attacked by an evil spirit outweighed any concern he had about letting his friends know he now believed in ghosts.

"It was wild and crazy, and for me it was strange because I was what you would call a conservative Republican business owner," he says. "But this experience really turned me around."

And the worst was still to come. Houser says one of the most terrifying encounters he experienced occurred one night just after he contacted the ghost buster. Andy was asleep in his bedroom. Then Houser heard him scream—a bloodcurdling, scared-for-your-life kind of scream.

"I ran out into the hallway. Andy was catatonic and I saw the evil spirit. Usually I could feel him, but this time I saw him, and he was chasing those ghost children down the stairs. I became very, very angry and took my fist and punched into the spirit and shouted, 'Get out of my house!' It laughed at me and began chasing the ghost children again. I grabbed Andy and we ran out of the house. As we got to the car Andy said, 'Dad, look at the house.' We saw the faces of two of the ghost children in the window looking very forlorn, like they didn't want us to leave."

The strange happenings escalated when the ghost buster, Echo Bodine, entered the home. Bodine was accompanied by a crew from the NBC show "The Other Side," which featured stories on the paranormal. The crew was filming Bodine as she went about her work in the house. The events that unfolded were far from staged, however.

For Bodine, it was a cold call. The renowned psychic did not allow her clients to tell her anything about their situation. And she had never set foot in the house before. As she walked from room to room, the lights in the home began flickering on and off. The electromagnetic meters brought in by Bodine's staff to detect electrical activity went off the charts. The mayhem was witnessed by 17 people, some from the television production crew, some from Bodine's staff and Houser's entire family, including his ex-wife.

Houser says Bodine detected the five ghost children right away. She also found the ghost of an old man in the basement whom she described as being very frail and very scared. "She said he was rocking back and forth and was a very faint spirit," Houser says. "Then she said, 'Over by the piano you have a very evil spirit.' And she shook."

As this was being captured on tape, the producer of "The Other Side" called the previous homeowner. She, too, had seen the ghost children and had been attacked by the evil spirit. In fact, that was the reason she had moved.

Bodine got down to the business of getting the spirits to move into the light. Houser and his family watched the events unfold on a live feed placed outside the house. "She asked the old man how long he'd been in the basement. He said about 15 years and that he didn't want to go into the light because he [was] looking for his wife. Echo told him that his wife had probably already gone into the light and that it was time for him to go, too."

After about 45 minutes of discussing the merits of heaven, Bodine finally convinced the ghost to turn around and walk into the light. "As he started to go, his son and then his wife came out of the light to get him," Houser says. "We were all picking this up from outside [by] watching their expressions."

Bodine then approached the ghost children. They didn't want to go into the light because they feared they would be separated. She placed a ball on the floor for them to play with. "She [told] them to go into the light and I could hear them talking but I couldn't understand what they were saying," Houser says. Andy translated for him. "They asked her if there were animals in heaven and she said, 'Yes.' "

And so Bodine coaxed the children into the light. The evil spirit wasn't so easy to convince, however. He refused to go into the light and he became menacing. "He said, 'I'm going to hell when it's my time,' " Houser recalls. "Echo was nervous and I could feel that this thing was very, very strong."

Bodine eventually opted to banish the spirit from the house. Her rebuke seemed to work; normalcy returned to the Houser home. For a short time anyway. Two months later, Houser's kids moved in with him full-time. Shortly after, the evil spirit returned home, too.

One cold January evening Houser went to the video store. When he returned he found the front door to his house open and his daughter and her friend locked in a hysterical huddle in a snowbank near the road. "My daughter was screaming that something was in the house, that Roger had showed up again," he says.

Houser became angry that the banishment hadn't been strong enough to keep Roger at bay. As he stood there wondering what to do, his neighbor came over and told him that he had power over the spirit. "I told her that I had had a professional here and she couldn't [even] deal with it," he says. "But she said I could rebuke the evil spirit with the power of faith in the spirit of God."

He scoffed at her and instead put the house up for sale, noting in his advertisement that the sale was because of a ghost. A week later, another woman approached him with the same message—that he could have power over the spirit through faith in the spirit of God.

The eerie coincidence prompted Houser to go to church. Soon he was attending twice a week and fervently studying the scriptures to learn about what is known as spiritual warfare.

In the meantime, Houser sold the house and bought another in the area. Things were good—life was settling down and his kids seemed happy. Until one evening when he returned home from church to find his children in a state of hysterics. Roger had followed them to their new home. "They said, 'Dad, he's back.' I said, 'Don't toy with me.' And they said, 'No, look out the window.' I did. He was hovering out there looking through the window at us."

Houser got down on his knees and starting praying. "I told him, 'I cast [you] out and rebuke you.' I kept repeating that for about 10 minutes. I had a strange feeling, almost like I was leaving my body. It was like I was in a trance. My son snapped me out of it. He said, 'Dad, look at the ceiling.' There were shadows moving all over the ceiling. I told Andy I couldn't see what they were. He said, 'They're angels, Dad, they're angels.' "

Houser now believes his family's encounters, which numbered more than 40 over the two years, were meant to lead him to the church. "The thought of losing my kids and not having them live with me scared me, but it also ignited something in me—faith," he says.

Houser is reformed in other ways, too. He now fully believes in ghosts and accepts that most, like the old man in his basement or the ghost children on the third floor, are lost spirits and basically harmless. He also believes there are spirits like Roger that are evil.

And Houser is convinced that nothing in life is a coincidence. Shortly after moving into his current home, he received a call from the Minnesota Historical Society. "They said the fence I have in my backyard is from the orphanage fire and would I like to donate it to the society," he says. "I told them to come and get it."

As for Lichliter, she now considers it proper to tell her clients any time there is a possibility the house they are about to buy is haunted. And she's more than willing to put them in touch with a ghost buster. "I do know that it had an impact on Mark and the kids that will never go away," she says. "They were spooked. This was not a minor deal and it rather consumed Mark. He's now going into the ministry."

A Never-ending Meeting Place

An old mansion on Manning Avenue North in Stillwater has been the center of town activity for more than 150 years. And from the amount of ghostly activity going on there today, it seems the home's reputation as a meeting place for town residents is still firmly intact.

Although no ghost has ever been seen, ghostly footsteps are heard regularly in the historic home.

The house was built in the 1850s and was a meeting place for both American Indians and Stillwater settlers. The attic served as a town hall and a social center for community dances.

Some think the ghost is that of William Rutherford, who helped found the settlement and lived in the house in the late 1800s.

Others believe a local legend that says an Indian who was killed in the upper story of the 10-room mansion is still stalking around. The ghostly footsteps seem to be confined to the upstairs of the house, leaving many convinced that the murdered American Indian is trying to find his way home.

The Floating Face

When it comes to haunted houses, an old farmhouse in the Collegeville-Avon area truly takes the cake. Neighbors say the overwhelming sense of foreboding emanating from the house is strong enough to be felt by passersby. And when someone new moves in, things get really frightening.

One resident of the old house reported being awakened in the night to find the disembodied head of a man suspended in a dark corner of his bedroom. The head was facing the frightened tenant and appeared to be watching him before it faded away.

Sometime later, the same tenant told staff at the Stearns History Museum that he heard a man's voice calling from the yard. When he went out to investigate, however, he found no one there.

Eventually the resident drew a picture of the face he saw and showed it to neighbors. Many thought the drawing bore a strong resemblance to the property's original owner, who died in a fierce storm.

The story goes that the original owner was enjoying some mid-winter cheer at a local bar. He accepted a dare from a fellow drinker to walk home in a blinding snowstorm. As he was walking he became disoriented and fell into a snow bank alongside the road, where he promptly fell asleep and froze to death.

His body was found by searchers the next day, his face frozen in anguish. Could it be the same face the renter saw that chilling night?

Spectral Knocking

A ghostly figure of a woman with long red hair wearing a 1930s-style chiffon dress is said to haunt an old house in St. Paul. The apparition reportedly rushes down the grand staircase in answer to a spectral knock on the front door.

One owner of the house reported this dramatic scene after falling victim to what she thought was a game of Knock Down Ginger. (Usually played by kids in the hours of darkness, the aim of this game is to ring a doorbell or knock loudly on a door, as though very urgent, and run away quickly.)

The owner was in the kitchen doing the dishes when she heard a rap on her front door. She went to see who was there and saw the ghostly redhead come sweeping down the stairs and out the door. Scared, she ran back into the kitchen. Seconds later another knock sounded. Still scared, she remained in the kitchen. The knocking grew louder and more impatient until finally the owner mustered up enough courage to open the door.

Standing there, looking very annoyed, was the owner's aunt. The aunt asked what took the owner so long to answer the door. Sensing that her aunt would not believe that she'd just seen a ghost, the owner asked her instead if she had seen anyone come out the front door. She replied that she was the only figure lurking in the doorway.

After this, the tenant would hear footsteps coming from the third floor of the house when she was home alone.

The owner's next encounter with a ghost in the house occurred one Christmas Eve. She had just finished putting toys under the Christmas tree and was sitting by the fire relaxing and reflecting when she was startled by the ghostly figure of a man in formal dress who walked through the living room window and appeared before her. He introduced himself as the builder of the house and said he was pleased that she lived there. He said he was glad she cherished the house as much as he had in life, and he wanted her to stay.

So stay she did. After all, who can refuse an invitation from a ghost?

Now the footsteps on the third floor aren't so scary, and neither is the knocking that comes from inside empty closet doors. Nothing untoward has ever happened to the owner in the home, leading her to believe that the spirit responsible for the footsteps and the knocking is pretty pleased with her as a housemate.

The Griggs Mansion

Most haunted houses lay claim to a single ghost. But the Griggs Mansion at 476 Summit Avenue in St. Paul is a veritable clearinghouse of spirits. The fabulous Romanesque-style stone mansion with its eerie skylight is reputed to be the most haunted house in the capital city, maybe even in the entire state.

The house was built in 1883 by Chauncey W. Griggs, a wholesale grocery tycoon. Griggs lived in the mansion for four years, until he moved to Tacoma to establish a lumber and transportation business. After that the home was turned into an art studio. Today it is the private residence of a woman who says she doesn't believe in ghosts. But the building's history is rife with spirits.

In 1915 a young servant, despondent over a love affair, supposedly hanged herself near the house's fourth-floor landing. Since her death, people in the home have reported a strong presence of suffering and sorrow. The first recorded case was in 1920 when a maid awoke to see a girl with long black hair wearing a white gown standing next to her bed. The ghost stretched out her hand to the terrified maid and then simply vanished.

Another ghost has been seen in the house's library. It is thought to be that of Charles Wade, the former gardener and caretaker of the house who spent his off-hours in the library reading his master's books.

Telltale signs of hauntings have also been reported in the house. Footsteps have been heard on empty staircases, doors have opened and closed by themselves, the sound of a rasping cough has come from empty rooms, lights have turned on and

Several specters have made the Griggs Mansion the spookiest house in St. Paul.

off by themselves and heavy drapes and objects have mysteriously moved when no one is near them.

In 1939 the Roger B. Shephard family donated the house to the St. Paul Gallery and School of Art. Teachers and students were uneasy in the house. They complained that it felt as if someone was watching them.

In the early 1950s, Dr. Delmar Kolb, a military intelligence officer during World War II, joined the staff at the institution and moved into a front basement apartment. He experienced several spooky encounters, and once the apparition of a tall thin man appeared suddenly in his room.

Kolb left St. Paul in 1959 and two college students took over his apartment. One awoke in the middle of the night to find a child's ghostly figure floating above his bed. Another felt cold, dead fingers pressed against his forehead. Figures with long bushy white hair, beards and top hats or other dress of the 19th century were regularly reported vanishing into walls or thin air.

The mansion was put up for sale when the new Arts and Sciences Center opened. It was purchased in 1964 by Carl Weschke, a publisher of occult books and the founder of Llewellyn Publishing, which publishes *FATE* magazine.

Weschke used the mansion as his production headquarters. He ordered massive renovations to the home and often stopped by to check on its progress. One day he found a window open on the upper floor and he closed it. The next day it was open again and he closed it again. The workmen claimed they had not touched the window, yet on the third day he checked and it was open again. Finally, Weschke nailed the window shut. But on his next visit, the window was open.

Weschke had other spooky experiences, too. On one occasion he saw an apparition of a man, and another time he says he was picked up by some invisible force and tossed into the air. He also reportedly heard odd noises at night, including footsteps going up and down the hallways and doors slamming shut.

Tales of the haunted house were so great that in February 1969 two hard-nosed reporters from the *St. Paul Pioneer Press* arranged to spend the night inside it to judge it for themselves. Staff writers Don Giese and Bill Farmer, along with photographer Flynn Ell, spent a terrifying evening on the third floor of the mansion, listening to footsteps marching up and down an empty staircase and feeling a terrifying sense of malevolence waiting for them.

At 4 AM the trio bolted out of the house through the back door, vowing never to set foot in the building again.

Flapjack Ghost

Jeremiah Leary died a wealthy bachelor in April 1905, after amassing more than 600 acres of prime agricultural land south of Willmar County. Jeremiah, or Jerry as he was fondly called, was known as a "thoroughly honest and upright man." It is said that he came back from the grave out of disgust over the bitter family squabble—led by his own brother no less—that broke out over the division of his estate.

The events of Jeremiah's death and his subsequent appearance as a ghost were chronicled in the now-defunct *Willmar Republican Gazette*. The following articles were passed along by Mona Nelson-Balcer, director of the Kandiyohi County Historical Society. These stories paint a fine picture of the scandal as it unfolded.

The first item ran in the April 13, 1905, edition of the *Willmar Republican Gazette* under the headline "Jerry Leary Dead."

Jerry Leary, one of the earliest settlers of this county, passed away at the home of his brother, Barney Leary, south of town, Sunday. Death was the result of an ailment of long-standing, but the decline towards the last was very rapid.

The funeral took place yesterday forenoon from St. Mary's Church of this city. Rev. Father J.J. Malloy was the officiating clergyman. The remains were interred in the Catholic cemetery just south of Willmar.

The deceased was born in St. Lawrence County, New York, 66 years ago, of sturdy Irish stock. He was engaged in the carpenter's trade in his native state until 1868, when he came west to Minnesota and took

a homestead south of Willmar. He was always an
industrious and frugal man, and accumulated a handsome lot of property, including about 600 acres of
land. He was never married.

Jerry Leary was known as a thoroughly honest and
upright man and one who would always lend a hand
to help a brother man. He is highly spoken of by all
who know him best. He leaves to mourn his death the
following brothers and sisters: Rev. John Leary of
Chapman, Kan.; Barney Leary, of this place; James
Leary, engineer on the Great Northern out of St. Paul;
Rev. M.A. Leary, of Chicago; Mrs. Liza Donovan, of
Graceville; Mrs. Charles Connelly, of St. Paul; Mrs.
Ellen Costello, of Minneapolis; and Miss Mary Leary,
of Chapman, Kan.

Jeremiah was barely in the ground when the fight broke
out over his estate. His brother Barney contested the will in
an effort to recoup expenses incurred while caring for the ailing bachelor. So much for brotherly love.

The next article appeared in the September 7, 1905, edition
of the *Willmar Republican Gazette* under the headline "A Ghost
in Town." It details Jeremiah's unusual return from the grave.

The Willmar correspondent for the *St. Paul
Dispatch* has evidently been overfed and is conse-
quently subject to hallucinations. Under date of
August 31, he sends in the following article under the
caption 'Wraith Bakes Pancakes.'

Last summer one of the old and respected citizens
of this community gathered to his fathers, a fine old
Irish gentlemen [sic], he was unmarried and wealthy.

He stayed with his brother in this city at the time of his death. One morning recently the wife of the house saw old Jerry, so she claims, standing by the kitchen stove baking pancakes.

The alleged visit of the departed occurred several times after that, always at the break of dawn, and the people are so frightened that they do not dare to live in the house. The Society for Psychic Research had better send a man to Willmar to investigate this supposed supernatural phenomenon.

The appearance of Jeremiah's ghost did little to deter the dispute over his estate. The matter came to a head in November when an unrepentant Barney and his wife took their claim for compensation to the courts.

The November 23, 1905, edition of the *Willmar Republican Gazette* captured this part of the story in an article entitled "Not Willing to Settle."

A meeting of the heirs of the late Jeremiah Leary was held in the judge of probate's office last Monday morning, and at this hearing an attempt was made to settle a claim that had been made by Mr. and Mrs. Barney Leary that would not be allowed by the interested parties for the amount asked.

The claim as made by Mr. Leary and wife asks for compensation in the amount of $4,306 for board, washing, mending of clothes, nursing and caring for the deceased for different periods of time starting from the year 1899.

Another claim is also put in by Mr. Leary for $198, expenses incurred while on a trip to the coast with the

deceased. Both of these claims were declared exhorbi-
tant [sic] by the other heirs in the case, and an offer was
made to the plaintiffs at this hearing to settle for
$1,000, but was not accepted.

Another hearing will be held before the judge of
probate on December 6 and if not settled then will
likely be taken to a higher court.

It is not known if Jeremiah's ghost ever showed up again.
Perhaps he knew what was good for him and he moved on to
his great reward, leaving his heirs to bicker over theirs.

Swensson Farm

It is sometimes said that truth is stranger than fiction. Such
is the case in the story of the Olof Swensson Farm near
Montevideo—depending, of course, on whose version of
truth you believe.

The Olof Swensson Farm is a museum made up of a 17-
acre farmstead located six miles east of Montevideo. It
includes a timber-frame barn built in the 1890s, the remains
of a horse-powered gristmill and a handful of old-fashioned
concrete tombstones made by Olof Swensson for the family
burial plot.

The house, which was built in 1901, rests on a foundation
of huge local granite stones, cut and laid in pattern by
Swensson and his daughter Katie. "Some of this granite is
4 feet thick and the foundation walls are 8 to 9 feet high,"
says June Lynne, director of the Chippewa County Historical
Society, current owner of the property. "For a father and
daughter to bring these massive pieces of granite from about

seven miles away by horse and wagon, cut them and lay them into place is an [amazing] feat."

The homestead is so impressive it is included on the National Register of Historic Places. It is also the source of much speculation. Some, like A.J. Cooper, a radio host at local radio station KRAM 96 FM, firmly believe the Olof Swensson Farm is haunted.

"[I've lived] in Monte[video] for a while and have [gone] to the Swensson Farm periodically, and I have heard stories of people driving by or neighbors seeing the lights flicker," Cooper says. "I also remember hearing a psychic from Europe saying the staircase…is haunted."

One of the wilder tales relayed by Cooper about the homestead has to do with a medical condition apparently suffered by the Swensson family. "Some of the Swenssons were diabetic and went into severe [blood sugar] comas," Cooper says. "So Olof built a tube from the burial plot on his land to his basement."

The idea was that if a family member was thought to be dead and was buried but was actually in a sugar coma Olof would hear him or her when he or she woke up and began shouting and banging in an attempt to get out of the coffin. "This is a very interesting place," says Cooper.

Not everyone buys into the homestead's spooky reputation, however. "I don't think that the Swensson Farm is haunted," Lynne says. "And as far as I know, there is nothing official…perhaps some normal noises that people 'hear' in a house that is not lived in."

Lynne also states, "There is no tunnel from the house to the family burial plot. If you saw the distance between the two, you would understand how that is simply not possible." She adds, "And as far as the staircase being haunted, this is the first I have heard of it."

2
Haunted Theaters & Museums

～

There's something about old theaters and hauntings that just seem to go hand in hand. Perhaps the baroque interiors, the red velvet seats and the gilt staircases that sweep grandly to the balconies create a sense of timelessness that spirits feel at home in. Museums are much the same, ageless buildings filled with rooms where time has purposely come to a full stop.

Many spirits return to the places that gave them the most joy in life, be it as a patron or a performer. Others are attracted to the settings where they felt most comfortable during life. Some spirits cling to treasured personal objects, such as family heirlooms, and stay with them wherever they end up, even if that place is an auction house or museum.

～

Long-term Usher

The Guthrie Theater in Minneapolis has been haunted for the past 35 years by the sad and lonely ghost of usher Richard Miller, a devoted former employee who requested in his suicide note that he be buried in his beloved usher's uniform.

Miller passed away on a bitterly cold February day in 1967, but Todd Hughes, box office manager at the Guthrie Theater, says his restless spirit "just never left aisle 18."

Aisle 18 is the longest aisle in the theater and the one with the most seats. It was Miller's domain for the two years he worked at the Guthrie seating patrons and watching performances. "Things move on aisle 18," Hughes says. "Chairs and programs move inexplicably and many people walking up and down the aisle say they feel that there is someone either right in front of them or behind them. It's a little freaky but not malicious in any way."

Miller's ghost is very much like what he was like in life. A loner with few friends and a scant social life, the University of Minnesota student struggled with failing grades. He reportedly suffered a nervous breakdown.

He quit his ushering job at the Guthrie on Saturday, February 15, 1967, and drove to Sears on East Lake Street where he purchased a gun. His body was found the following Monday, slumped over in the driver's seat of his car in the Sears parking lot, dead of an apparent self-inflicted gunshot wound to the head. He was still wearing his Guthrie usher's uniform.

Shortly after his death, a woman sitting in aisle 18 wrote a letter to theater staff complaining about an usher pacing during a performance. The woman described the restless staff member, and the description fit Miller perfectly, right down to the large mole on his cheek.

In 1968, Scott Herner hid in the theater with two other ushers, Ouija board in hand. They set up on the thrust stage and by candlelight asked the board some questions. They received a message instructing them to look up to the lighting booth for a ghost the board identified as DIKMILER. Herner, who hadn't known Miller, didn't think much of it. But both his companions, who had worked with Miller, were terrified.

When they looked up at the lighting booth, the transparent figure of a man standing behind the lighting board could clearly be made out. Even more horrifying was that the figure was wearing a blue jacket with a red breast pocket—the standard usher's uniform at the Guthrie.

Later, two ushers working late heard a piano playing on stage. When they looked towards the stage the piano was there but the player was not.

From then on the ghostly figure was seen by ushers with alarming regularity. He made appearances in the catwalks above the theater, in the queen's box, in a section with the best seats in the house, in the freight elevator and in the vom tunnel that runs directly underneath aisle 18 and exits to the left and right of the stage.

It wasn't only ushers who saw Miller's ghost. A lighting technician exiting the elevator reported seeing a transparent figure. An actor reported that the ghost appeared suddenly in her car as she drove past the theater. And another actor claimed that she saw an usher materialize in the seats while she rehearsed in an otherwise empty theater.

Miller's ghost has also been credited with the mysterious movements of several props, doors and lighting equipment on stage.

The hauntings continued until 1993, at which time an Anishinabe Indian elder was hired to perform a spiritual cleansing of the building before its grand reopening. The elder reported a presence that was male, then he conducted a ceremony to send the spirit to the spirit world. No one has seen the ghost usher since.

And no one may ever see the ghost again, as the Guthrie Theater will be torn down in 2003 when the new Guthrie Arts Center is complete.

The ghost of an usher who loved working here is thought to be putting in many extra hours at the Guthrie Theater.

Christopher the Mischievous

The Performing Arts Center at Winona State University has hosted its share of productions over the years, but none can hold a candle to the theatrics of its mischievous resident ghost, Christopher.

Christopher's ghostly presence lingers in and around the stage lighting booth and is blamed for setting off much mayhem—sometimes even during live productions—by turning the stage lights off and on, opening and closing the stage doors and moving props and equipment.

Over the years, members of the Wenonah Players, a student theater company, have reportedly encountered Christopher during rehearsals and performances. But staff members say he is most active at night. Christopher's favorite haunt appears to be the main stage—and with good reason. That is where he passed away.

Winona State University acting student Christopher Robb Neidringhaus died on October 6, 1973, a day after he was found lying unconscious in a broken heap on the floor of the Performing Arts Center's main theater.

Documents at WSU say that Christopher, who went by the nickname "Christopher Robb N" and later "Christopher Robin" after the A.A. Milne character, had fallen 80 feet from the catwalk some time during the evening of October 5. There was some confusion as to whether he fell from the stage left gallery or the stage right storage gallery. In any event, he never regained consciousness, and he died from internal bleeding mid-afternoon the following day.

The WSU documents say that at the request of Christopher's parents, Carl and Christina Neidringhaus, the accident was never investigated or the cause pursued, "perhaps in order to avoid the discovery that it was a suicide." In interviews with the police, Christopher's roommate and other friends divulged that the shy, quiet and reserved student had been despondent and depressed for some time and "probably" into drugs.

The Performing Arts Center hauntings began in June 1974, about eight months after Christopher's unfortunate death. Some at PAC attributed the haunting to the acting student because June is the sixth month of the year and Christopher died on the sixth day of October. Others noted that after Christopher's death the roof suddenly stopped leaking on the side of the stage where he lay at death's door, and that bees or wasps refused to light on that side of the stage.

Today, nervous janitors complain of strange scuffling noises coming from the rows of seats as they clean the darkened theater. They prefer to exit through the theater's rear door and walk all the way around the building just to avoid leaving by the front door, which would necessitate turning off all the lights and crossing the theater in total darkness.

Lights appear to be Christopher's favorite means of getting attention. The PAC was struck with myriad mysterious lighting problems in the year after Christopher's death, primarily with the lighting board. Staff say whenever the ghost played with the lighting board, lights would flicker, blink and shake. When someone went to investigate, the board itself was almost always found to be in the "C" preset mode, "C" as in Christopher.

Today that lighting board has been replaced by a lighting booth, but the change of setting doesn't seem to have deterred Christopher's antics. Indeed when he's not scaring employees in the main stage area by causing lights to suddenly sputter and burn out, Christopher shifts to the Dorothy B. Magnus Theater. There he is accused of making a light flicker on and off during the play *Eleemosynary*, only to have it stay lit through intermission.

Christopher seems to affect lights wherever he goes. Along the catwalk there is one light that doesn't work properly, even though there is nothing mechanically wrong with it. It shakes, bounces and blinks, frustrating the stage crew to no end.

In one desperate attempt to pacify Christopher, the stage crew placed a chair, now called "Christopher's chair," under the temperamental light. Evidently the gesture was well received, for the light began working perfectly. When the chair was moved or someone sat in it, the lights malfunctioned again.

Christopher has never been seen, but he has been heard. A former staff member working alone in the lighting booth late one night was startled to hear someone say, "Hi." Shortly after, a student working in the main stage area reported hearing footsteps on the catwalk—the same catwalk from which Christopher fell to his death. Even creepier is that there was no way anyone could have climbed up the noisy metal staircase to the catwalk undetected—anyone human, anyway.

WSU students appear to sense Christopher's presence the most, and some student actors claim he communicates with them. Once, when one such group of students on the main stage started to talk about the ghost, an eerie glow shone from the lighting booth and strange creaks and groans were heard throughout the PAC. When they discussed his death, the phenomena grew more intense. And when they changed the subject, it stopped.

Christopher is the source of so much weirdness at the PAC that there's even a bravery award named after him. It's given to the employee who spends the most time at the theater.

Art Is Here

The Rochester Repository Theater is haunted by a ghost that, though rarely seen, makes its presence known loud and clear.

"Things happen here for which there are apparently no explanations," says local actor Cheryl Frarck. "My associates and I admit the theater is haunted, but we certainly don't [go out of our way to] publicize it because we have jobs to hold."

Frarck says that when the ghost does appear, it's in the form of an older man dressed in coveralls. It stands near the doorway leading to the backstage area of the theater. But it's when the ghost is not showing itself that Frarck gets the creeps. "It's not a bad feeling, it's not a scary feeling, it's not a terrifying feeling, it's just a feeling that I'm not alone," she says. "Other people have described it, too. It's a sense of being watched."

The theater company moved into the second floor of the repository building in 1984. Built in the 1860s, the historic building is one of the oldest in Rochester and is on the National Register of Historic Places. It has a unique history. At one time it housed a butcher shop on the first floor and an undertaker's parlor on the second.

Frarck had her first encounter with the ghost she calls Art while watching a rehearsal for *The Glass Menagerie*. She was sitting in the theater when she felt an uncomfortable vibration in her fold-down seat. "It was as if someone was walking up the steps to the platform," she says. "Over the course of the night I moved three or four times because it happened again and again."

One time when Frarck changed positions she saw a seat two away from her own fold down, as if someone were joining her in watching the rehearsal. "I turned and looked and the seat was down," she says. "I [cried out in surprise] and the actors asked what was wrong. I said, 'Call me crazy, but I think Art's here and he just sat down.' Then [they] started talking about [their] experiences."

Frarck says it was a relief to learn she wasn't the only one to have a run-in with Art. She recalls some of the stories the others told her.

In one incident, one of the volunteers was leaning against a wall watching a performance. The box office was on the other side of the wall, and the woman could plainly hear what sounded like moving chairs coming from there. The noise was so loud that she became annoyed and walked around to the office intending to lambaste whoever was responsible for it. When she got there, however, no one was there.

In another incident, an electrician was working alone in the building rewiring the lighting system. Following theater policy, he had locked all the doors. No one could get in. Yet when the man was working up in an area overlooking the stage, he saw someone standing under the "exit" sign. The electrician yelled down at him, asking him who he was and what he was doing there, but he got no answer. The electrician ran down the steps just in time to see the man turn and walk into the back area of the theater. When the electrician caught up to where the man should be, no one was there.

The electrician called the president of the theater company and told him that there was a man in the building but he couldn't find him. He asked the president to come down to help him search. The electrician described the visitor as an older man wearing coveralls.

Frarck recounts another incident that occurred when she was alone in the theater painting props late one night. She, too, had locked herself in the building, so she knew she was the only one there. "I heard a door slam," she says. "I was so scared it was to the point that the hair on my arms started to stand up. I said, 'Art, I think I'm going to go home now,' and I cleaned up my brushes and left."

Some encounters have occurred during the day. For instance, in the early 1990s the president of the theater group received a panicked call from the box office coordinator at 2:30 PM. "She said she knew someone was in the theater even though the door was locked," Frarck recalls. "She said she could hear someone moving around. The president came down and helped her search the place but they couldn't find anyone. This happened to her several times and it got to the point that if she was alone in the theater she never left the box office."

Unexplained incidents have occurred during performances, too. One time the troupe had borrowed a vintage 1950s jukebox to use as a prop during the production of *Sea Horse*. The owner of the jukebox had packed its mechanisms carefully in foam as the jukebox would not be operational during the play but only plugged in for a lighting effect.

In the play Frarck's character was to unplug the jukebox to stop the music, which was actually being fed in through the sound system. On this particular night, however, Frarck was on stage when she suddenly heard a whirring sound coming from inside the jukebox. Having seen that the inner workings of the jukebox had been packed away in foam, Frarck knew it was impossible that the jukebox should work.

Yet in the next scene, when Frarck was sitting down talking with another character, the jukebox turned on and began blaring music. It was playing "Help" by the Beatles. Frarck deviated from the script and got up and unplugged the jukebox. The music stopped and the play continued.

Later, as the director and actors were trying to figure out what went wrong, Frarck went over to the jukebox and went through the playlist. "I went down the line and not a single one of those records were Beatles records," she says. "When the jukebox's owner heard about it, he thought maybe one of the records had jiggled loose. But I was standing right there when he removed the back, and there wasn't anything loose. It was all still in the foam packing."

Many of these incidents occurred 10 years ago, but Frarck says other things have happened more recently. Two years ago a letter arrived at the theater addressed simply to "Art at the Rochester Repository Theater." The return address showed it was from the building's owner.

"The box office attendant that summer was a student and he brought the letter back asking who Art was," Frarck says. "He'd worked there for two summers and knew there wasn't anybody working there by that name. He kept asking, so I finally told him that Art was the resident ghost. He didn't believe me. Just then, coming from the men's washroom we heard the distinctive sound of the paper towel dispenser being used, but we were the only people in the theater. That particular time it was as if Art was saying, 'Yeah, I'm here.'"

Art also wished the actors some Christmas cheer one year—in his own ghostly way, of course. After a performance the ensemble was cleaning up the lobby, putting Christmas decorations away. One of them said they were going over to take down the tree, which was beside the refreshment bar. The front of the refreshment bar was decorated with a swag of tinsel with Christmas bulbs hanging from it.

Suddenly, the group heard a clink, Frarck says. "They turned to find a glass Christmas bulb on the bar. One of the guys said he saw the ball fall onto the bar from the corner of his eye. He said it was like the ball had been dropped, but it didn't bounce or roll or break."

Frarck says the group began talking about where the ball could have come from. The man who saw the ball said he assumed it had come from the tinsel on the front of the refreshment bar, which, of course, was hanging below the top of the bar.

Another ensemble member saw a man in coveralls go into the cloakroom. Frarck says he called for the figure to stop and then chased after him. No one was in the cloakroom when he got there.

The sheer number of ghostly incidents in the theater has led volunteers to consult paranormal investigators, Frarck says. Photos taken during one of these sessions show orbs, or spirit lights, and streaks of energy in the theater, the tech room and the green room.

A psychic has also identified the spirit of a young man, likely developmentally disabled, and the energy of an older man in the building. But he isn't named Art. "The psychic said something about the river, which is right out back of the theater," Frarck says. "I got the impression this person was more a vagrant than it was Art."

Over the years Frarck and her troupe have learned to coexist with the Rochester Repository Theater ghost. It is now more or less policy to not work alone in the building.

But when they do, Frarck says, it's almost comforting to hear the paper towel dispenser being used or a door slamming shut or to just the sense that someone is hanging around. "If the hair on my arms begins standing up, it's time to go home to bed. But I have never felt threatened. If anything, I have felt like I was interfering for being in his theater."

Ben and Veronica

Of the many ghosts that haunt the Fitzgerald Theater in downtown St. Paul, the one called Ben is the most active.

Ben is thought to be the spirit of an old stagehand who worked the lights back in 1910 when the building was known as the Schubert Theater. He started appearing in 1985 as the Fitzgerald underwent renovations.

The Fitzgerald Theater is haunted by ghosts that are usually—but not always—friendly.

The sightings began when workmen removed the salon ceiling and discovered a secret balcony that had been sealed off from the rest of the theater. At the same time they unearthed a note to a stage worker named Ben.

Almost immediately staff complained of unexplained cold spots and reported a shadowy figure lurking about the recesses of the theater. In addition, empty and dusty antique bottles of muscatel wine started to appear, and tools went missing or were mysteriously moved from one part of the theater to another.

The theater manager claimed she saw a ghostly man standing at the workshop with a workman's uniform on. She watched as he walked right through the brick wall that leads on to Wabasha Street. She found out later that that spot is located where the original door of the theater was.

The Fitzgerald is now the home base of Garrison Keillor's popular radio program "A Prairie Home Companion." And Ben's presence is mostly benign, although one incident tinged with malevolence has caused staff to be wary of the ghost.

In that incident, two theater employees were walking through the backstage area using a flashlight to light their path. Without warning, a large chunk of plaster plummeted to the floor between them, missing their heads by mere inches. As the startled employees turned their flashlights upwards to see what had happened, they saw a shadowy figure moving swiftly along the catwalks before vanishing into thin air.

The employees could easily have blamed the accident on faulty construction. The problem with that explanation is that the ceiling in the Fitzgerald is not made of plaster. But the ceiling in the Schubert was.

A ghost called Veronica is also reluctant to leave the Fitzgerald Theater. Believed to be the spirit of an actress who performed at the theater many years ago, Veronica is often heard loud and clear. The sound of her singing frequently resonates in the auditorium at night after the lights go down. And theater staff don't mind her music, at least not as much as they mind the red lipstick smooches she is known to leave on mirrors in the dressing rooms and lobby.

Jokes by George

Lakeshore Players Community Theater in White Bear Lake is Minnesota's oldest theater. Housed in a magnificent steepled church built in 1890, Lakeshore is in its 49th season. It has entertained local audiences since the mid-1950s.

Actors of all stripes come to the theater located at Sixth Street and Stewart Street to take part in the three plays staged each season. And some get more than they bargained for if George, the ghost said to haunt Lakeshore Players Community Theater, decides to make an appearance.

George is prone to harmless pranks, such as moving power tools around and hiding them as staff are busy building props and scenery. And according to actor Deborah Frethem, George is very protective of women.

Frethem worked at the theater a few years ago during the run of a musical comedy about macabre murders of the 1940s. Sensitive to spirits and ghosts, Frethem picked up on George's presence immediately. "He seemed to develop a liking for me," she says. "He would move my costume pieces around and I'd later find them hanging up in the light booth."

George is also opposed to violence, Frethem says. She recalls one particularly intense scene in the play where another female character was supposed to threaten her with a knife. The knife was a prop, but that didn't seem to matter to George.

"No matter where she [the actor] put the knife beforehand, she could never find it during the play to threaten me with," Frethem says. The woman started hiding the prop in secret spots, but it still went missing. And after much searching, it would turn up in the strangest places. "One time they even found it out back of the theater in the dumpster," Frethem says.

But Frethem discovered a dark side to George, too. Or perhaps there is a second ghost, a more dangerous ghost, also haunting the old church.

In the theater's second year Frethem was cast as a prostitute in the play *British Don't Like Sex*. The props for her costume included a bullwhip and a riding crop, which she left upstairs in a storage area. "On opening night I went upstairs to get the props. I couldn't find the light switch, so I went in the dark," she says. When she reached the third step, a light in the loft started to glow faintly. "It grew very, very bright, then it went out," she says. "As that happened I felt this cold, cold presence coming down the stairs at me and it was malevolent. I was scared for my life."

Frethem says she ran back down the staircase and got someone else to go up to the loft to retrieve her props. Evidently this person didn't have a problem, as the show went off without a hitch. Frethem, however, never went upstairs again.

James Patrick (J.P.) Barone, president of the theater's board of directors, says he's heard only a vague reference to a ghost. "I checked with Lakeshore's office manager, Sherrie Tarble, who has worked in the building for 20 years," he says. "Although she has not had personal experience with the ghost, she has heard stories from people who have done volunteer work late at night, building sets, rehearsing, etc. The stories relate to shadows on the stairs and strange noises."

Barone adds that the name George was chosen at random and does not relate to any particular person. While his information about ghostly happenings is a far cry from what Frethem says she's experienced, Barone thinks he has an explanation. "The tall steeple and traditional design lends itself to a ghostly look," he says. "Also, a building that is 111 years old will have noises and shadows that are subject to various explanations."

Ghostly Mother

The historic Warden's House in Stillwater is said to be haunted by the ghost of a young woman looking after her infant son.

Various psychics have on separate occasions identified a spirit living on the upper floor of the structure as "Trudy," a name that holds significant historical meaning at the Warden's House, according to Brent Peterson of the Washington County Historical Society.

The Warden's House was built in 1853 just south of the Minnesota Territorial Prison. It is the only building that survives from the old jail. It is now home to the Washington County Historical Museum.

Although the spirit living in the house could belong to any number of the female prisoners of old, Peterson believes it is that of Gertrude Wolfer Chambers, the daughter of Henry Wolfer, the last warden to have lived in the house. Gertrude, or Trudy as she was called, was nine years old when the Wolfer family moved into the warden's house. She grew up in the home and lived there until she married.

Trudy and her husband moved to Blue Earth, Minnesota, after their wedding and there she gave birth to a son. Eight months later Trudy died of "inflammation of the bowels," or appendicitis, leaving her infant son behind. Peterson says the boy was taken in by his maternal grandfather and spent the first years of his life living in the Warden's House before moving out west with the family.

Is Gertrude Wolfer Chambers still taking care of the beloved eight-month-old son she left behind? Psychics seem to think so.

"Early last year [2000] a group of psychics came through the museum and felt that some 'energy' was present and they asked to come back during nonpublic hours," says Peterson. "When they returned, all of them felt that there was a young woman upstairs. This woman was fussing over a baby and would move between rooms. One person felt this woman was suffering from pain in the stomach. With that these people left."

Later that summer, another woman approached the museum. Peterson says she told staff members that there was still someone living in the house.

The presence of a ghost worrying over a baby has been felt in this museum, which used to be a warden's house.

"We told her the house has been a museum for nearly 60 years and that nobody has lived in the house since then," Peterson says. "She told us it was a spirit of a young woman who once lived there many years ago. When this person entered the house and went upstairs into what is called the children's room, she felt the presence of this spirit and found out that it was her baby she was caring for and that her name was Trudy. It's strange that two sets of psychics came at different times and said the same things."

Evidently Trudy's spirit came to rest at the place she loved best in life, her happy childhood home. And it turns out hers is not the only one. Peterson says the group of psychics also said they saw or "felt" a presence downstairs and that it was a man in a gray-looking uniform.

"This would have been a 'trustee' convict working in the house," he says. "And some of the psychics said there was another man like that outside near the carriage house. I'm unsure about these, though."

Ambitious Apparitions

When it comes to ghosts, the Mantorville Theater has got it all.

There's the figure of a sad old woman dressed in black, which usually appears after a rustle of long skirts is heard. There's the phantom that steals props and creates general mischief. And there's the apparition that loves to torment the actors by playing with the lights, especially in the middle of the night long after the theater is closed up for the evening.

"The police often call to say we left all the lights on in the building," says Cheryl Frarck, a director at the theater. "They're thinking we aren't turning the lights off when, in fact, it's the ghosts."

That the theater should contain ghosts is not at all surprising. Mantorville is named after brothers Peter and Riley Mantor, who arrived in the area in 1853. The building is located in the midst of a 12-block area of downtown that was listed on the National Register of Historic Places in 1975 because of its wealth of architectural heritage.

The area's architectural legacy stems from the material used in its buildings, a local limestone called Mantorville Stone, which was in high demand for its beauty and its unique response to the weather. When mined, the stone was very soft and easily worked into buildings, bridges and roads. With each passing year, it became harder as it endured the elements.

Mantorville Stone is responsible for the beauty of a variety of famous buildings still in use today, including the Dodge County courthouse, which is the oldest working courthouse in Minnesota, and the Hubbell House.

Built in 1856, the Hubbell House is an elegant restaurant of Early American and Civil War atmosphere. It is also haunted. It is said that people who come in to clean are always tripping over a little old lady who is there but not there.

But the Mantorville Theater has by far the most interesting ghosts. One evening Frarck, who also directs at the Rochester Repository Theater just three miles away, shut down the theater and walked to a bar across the street for a drink. When she came out again at around eleven thirty that night, she noticed something odd. "The light was on in the men's dressing room and I knew I had shut it off," she says.

Frarck returned to the theater and walked upstairs to the dressing room. When she got there, however, the lights were off. She trudged back downstairs and out of the theater, locked the door again and headed to her car. When she looked back at the building, the light in the men's dressing room was on again.

Frarck was flabbergasted. "I can't tell you how many times that has happened at Mantorville, and I know it has happened to other directors, too," she says.

Frarck has also fallen victim to a ghostly game of prop switching at Mantorville. She was playing a character for which one of the props was granny-style eyeglasses. In between performances Frarck kept the glasses in the pocket of her apron, thinking it was the safest place to leave them.

"One night I got to the theater and got my costume on and reached into the pocket and the glasses weren't there," she says. "We looked all over for the glasses and couldn't find them, so finally I resorted to using a supplemental pair."

During the production, in a scene where Frarck was playing opposite a villain, the villain was supposed to pull out a rolled-up deed from the inside breast pocket of his jacket. Frarck says he pulled something out all right. "Guess what he pulled out of his pocket?" she says. "The missing glasses were wrapped in the deed."

Another ghostly prank involved paint chips found in clean mugs used as props during a production of *Sweeney Todd*. "[One] particular actor had a habit of washing the cups he used as props in the show right before the play, and it was no different this time," Frarck says. "It came time to pour the drinks and the two actors took a sip and start making these strange faces. It turns out someone had sprinkled paint chips into both clean mugs in the space of about 20 minutes."

One of the scariest incidents at the Mantorville Theater occurred after a show when a group of cast members were preparing to leave the building. "The four of us were talking and suddenly clear as a bell there was the sound of heavy boots like a man's footsteps right above our heads upstairs walking down the hallway and stopping at the top of the stairs," Frarck says. "It was real. All of us heard it."

The group was sure no one else was in the building. "No one was up there and the lights were all off, so we decided it was time to go home," Frarck says. "I did not even have the interest to look back to see if the lights were on."

Mystery in the Museum

I first heard about the haunting of the Hennepin History Museum from John Brewer of the *Southwest Journal* in Minneapolis. Brewer had written a few articles about the museum, which is housed in the George Christian Mansion in Whittier. He suggested that the museum's curator, Jack Kabrud, might have a story or two to share.

Kabrud confirmed that he has experienced plenty of strange happenings in his 16 years at the museum. However, he says he's no closer to explaining any one of them than the day he walked in the door.

"The stories and experiences relating to the Hennepin History Museum are ones shared mostly by staff, volunteers and some visitors," Kabrud says. "There is a remarkable consistency to these experiences; however, we don't seem to be able to confirm any deaths or other such events [that happened] in the house that would typically be connected to ghostly experiences."

Whatever is haunting the Hennepin History Museum attracts attention with a variety of pranks.

Kabrud says many people have reported a broad range of odors in the building, from a very distinctive barnyard smell to pipe smoke to perfumes. These scents come and go very quickly, he says, and are totally unrelated to patrons visiting the museum. Isolated pockets of cold or warm air have also been reported in the building, Kabrud says, and he himself has, on occasion, heard snatches of conversation.

Women feel the phenomena more than men, Kabrud says, noting that many female patrons have experienced the feeling that someone is very near to them. When they turn around, however, no one is there. "[Women] have also been more inclined to feel threatened or a sense of discomfort connected to the experience," he says.

But Kabrud says none of these ghostly encounters compares to the unsettling occurrence he witnessed a couple of years ago. "My own most startling experience occurred in the autumn of 2000. I happened to be passing my own office door when a noise in my office caught my attention. When I walked in to see what was up, I noticed the water spinning rapidly round and round inside the drinking water dispenser. I stood there for almost a half a minute watching, and truly felt the hair on my neck stand on end. Finally the spinning slowed down, but the surface of the water continued to vibrate for a considerable time."

Kabrud adds, "These are, I suppose, rather mundane experiences as such things go. But when you are the person experiencing them they don't seem so mundane."

Kabrud says the museum artifacts date back to the 18th century, and it's possible that many of them carry a piece of their previous owners with them. "There's clearly something, these things are fairly consistent and baffling," he says. "Because of the nature of the museum and its collection, I don't feel it has to be the spirit of some dead person from here."

Area 35

Most of the unexplained events at the Minneapolis Institute of the Arts occur in Area 35. Many visitors report feeling ill at ease in this third-floor section where period furnishings and works of art are kept. Young children often become sick there and teenage girls get light-headed and faint with alarming regularity.

While security guards publicly attribute the incidents to overtired kids and stuffy, recycled air, privately some believe the phenomena are caused by a clash of spirits frustrated over their detachment from cherished family belongings that are in the display.

Ghosts definitely populate Area 35, as security guard Desmond Griffin can attest. One day, Griffin was gazing out a window in Area 35 watching the activity going on below. Though he had been alone on the floor moments earlier, he saw from the corner of his eye a woman coming down the hallway towards him.

Griffin figured the woman was coming to ask for directions and so he decided to wait until she reached him rather than walk over to her. She was about two steps away when he turned towards her. "I said, 'Hello, may I help you?' " he says. "But there was nobody there."

Another unexplained incident took place one evening as a guard was working late to finish some last-minute paperwork. The lights were off in the museum as he left his third-floor office near the Period Room in Area 35 and made his way down the long darkened hallway to the main stairwell.

But every time the guard approached a dark, shadowy spot in the hallway the lights would suddenly turn on—only to turn off again just as quickly when he reached a lit portion of the hallway. This activity followed the terrified guard even as he picked up his pace and ran out of the building, fully aware that no such light control existed anywhere in the building.

But perhaps the most unnerving incident took place one night during a graveyard shift. A guard was in the control booth watching monitors for any suspicious activity. Around 3:30 AM he began to get very sleepy and dozed off—but not for long. He was roused from his slumber by a light tapping noise on the control booth window.

The tapping grew louder and more insistent until the guard was finally fully awake. When he looked through the window to see who was there, he saw a ghostly figure of an old woman in a cream silk wedding dress. He recognized the figure immediately as the subject of an oil painting entitled *Mrs. T* hanging on the third floor.

The guard watched incredulously as Mrs. T waved her finger back and forth at him, as if scolding him with a "No, No, No," and then walked through the locked door to the control booth, passed by him and vanished. He hasn't worked a night shift since.

Spooky Spectators

More than one actor performing at the Chanhassen Dinner Theaters building over the past 20 years has come to suspect that he or she is sharing the stage with something other than great talent.

The Fireside Theater, one of four theaters at the Chanhassen, is said to be haunted by the ghost of a 1900s farmwoman and that of a red-clad patron who suffered a heart attack in her seat minutes before the opening night of the play *Loot* in 1978.

Attending paramedics tried to revive the ailing woman in red on the stage before putting her in the ambulance. She died en route to the hospital. Two days later, when theater management found out about the death, the curtain was brought down on *Loot* for good. Unfortunately, the play was a black comedy with a plot that revolved around hiding a woman's dead body.

Since then, everyone from actors to cleaning staff have claimed to witness a woman wearing red seated in the front row of the theater, as if waiting to watch the performance death cheated her out of seeing.

"I actually had a cleaner tell me she didn't clean in the theater because there was a woman in red sitting in there," says Fireside Theater production stage manager Susan Magnuson, who doesn't believe in ghosts. "I…told her it probably had more to do with the fact that some of our seats are reddish in color."

The cleaner insisted that she had seen a woman sitting there and refused to go back in. And Magnuson says several other employees won't enter the Fireside Theater either.

"I have never seen anything there and I'm there all the time," she says. "But odd things have happened in that space. If lights are going to malfunction, they will malfunction in there. Or lights will come on when you walk into the room when no one is in the lighting booth. [Or] the color wheel will turn on and fade out when no one is near the controls."

The ghost of the farmwoman in the Fireside Theater stems from a sighting that occurred in 1984 or 1985 during the run of a musical called *Quilters. Quilters* told the story of a pioneer mother and her five daughters, and how the women of that era made quilts to tell the tales of their joys, hardships and sorrows.

Shortly after the opening of the play, two of the actors reported feeling the presence of a spirit on stage with them, says Kris Howland, Chanhassen Dinner Theaters publicist.

"One of the actors actually saw the spirit move with them as they danced on stage," she recalls. "She was an older lady in a pioneer-style dress. Shortly thereafter, I believe someone brought in a psychic medium to conjure the spirit or to establish whether a presence was there. I think the medium felt a presence but no connection was made."

Magnuson, who was stage manager for that particular production, recollects this incident also. "Some of the actresses said they swore they could see a woman on the stage dressed as they were, which was Victorian style," she says, "except that they could see her in the negative, so to speak, in a whitish or grayish color."

Howland notes that around the time all of this was going on, Britta Bloomberg, the daughter of the owners of the Chanhassen Dinner Theaters, came across a newspaper article about a pioneer woman named Mary who had lived on the farm that used to be on the corner of the dinner theaters' property. With the article was a photo of Mary standing by the old farmhouse.

"Mary lived to see the construction of the dinner theaters and died a few years later," Howland says. "When the picture was shown to the cast members that had experienced encounters, they thought the spirit was Mary. And so she was named Mary Ole."

Magnuson, however, believes that Mary is just a figment of some overactive imaginations. She believes that the actors were actually seeing optical illusions, the result of working under bright lights on a darkened stage, similar to the "ghosting" effect one gets from seeing a bright flash of light. "It would always happen when they were turning around at the end of a scene," she explains.

Howland has a similar opinion about the two Fireside Theater ghosts. "No one really knows," she says. "Since that time [1984 or 1985] no employee or guest has experienced an encounter."

Howland adds that many other ghost stories attached to the Chanhassen Dinner Theaters are "inflated from a tiny piece of reality that gets exaggerated over and over until very little truth exists." Case in point is a published story that identifies a specific ghost as Marjorie, an actress said to have played the pioneer mother in *Quilters*. The story goes that Marjorie was hit and killed by a car while riding her bicycle home from the production, the only one she ever performed in at Chanhassen.

Magnuson says this story is incorrect. To begin with, Marjorie never appeared on stage, Magnuson says. And although she was killed while riding her bicycle, it was long after the theater dropped the final curtain on *Quilters*.

"She was riding her bicycle and didn't have a helmet on," she says. "The family decided to disconnect [the life support system she was on] because of brain damage. Had you known Marjorie, that story [of her returning as a ghost] really wouldn't make sense. She was a very logical, no-nonsense kind of girl."

Magnuson also points to a story involving the theater dresser, Barbara Ordahl, and a waitress. The waitress was working upstairs in the dining room, an enclosed room where people could catch a bite to eat before the show and then walk downstairs to their seats. She was going about her business when in the darkened back of the room she saw a ghost standing by the stairs that ran down to the back stage.

The waitress "screamed and ran down the stairs, saying she'd seen a shadowy figure with a white halo," Magnuson recalls. "I didn't find out about the story until several weeks later. About the same time, my dresser, Barbara, who has a lovely head of white hair, told me that she had gone up the back stairs in the dark to empty something in the sink up there. She said she couldn't figure out why the waitress looked at her and screamed and ran down the stairs. So in this case the ghost was Barbara with her stunning head of white hair."

Magnuson may not believe in ghosts but she does admit she's witnessed her fair share of unexplained phenomena over the years. One of those incidents took place at the now-defunct The Other Place Theater housed in the old Harmon Mansion, which was torn down to make way for the Metropolitan.

In The Other Place Theater a room on the second floor was used as a wardrobe. When Magnuson was working in there she would hear people walking on the staircase. "[But] when I'd look out, there would be no one but me in the building," she says. "I must admit that building felt odd."

Magnuson also worked at the original Guthrie Theater and admits there was definitely "something there" too.

Invisible Apparition

Though no one has ever seen a ghost at the Le Sueur County Historical Society Museum, enough strange and unexplained events have occurred there that employees are convinced the historic 1895 brick schoolhouse the museum calls home is haunted by a mischievous spirit.

Museum staff members have witnessed a phonograph start playing by itself and old-fashioned typewriters typing by themselves, and they've heard voices in various parts of the museum when only one person is at work.

Located in Elysian, the eerie-looking schoolhouse is open to the public from May to September, leaving staff to wonder exactly what goes on behind closed doors during the seven months the museum is closed.

The museum office is located on the second floor of the schoolhouse. Visitors must press a buzzer at the street-level front door to get in, letting staff know that they have arrived.

On one occasion, three staff members were up in the office working by the computer when they heard the old-style hotel bell kept at the main-floor reception area ring. No one else was in the building at the time; had anyone come in the workers would have heard the buzzer. Moreover, nothing could have fallen on the bell to make it ring.

In another incident, two staff members were giving a tour of one of the museum's exhibits, which included an antique stereopticon (kind of like a Viewmaster). One of the staff members set the artifact back down in its usual spot, then both employees left the exhibit. Five minutes later, the employees returned to find the stereopticon had been moved. Yet no one else had been in the room.

The strange thing about these ghostly events is that they do not happen on a regular basis. In fact, there are usually only about two occurrences during the museum's five-month season.

A playful spirit sporadically haunts this old schoolhouse.

3
Spirits
on the
Menu

With the number of restaurants and pubs that are established in old and historic homes and buildings, it should come as no surprise that these spots are a popular haunt for spirits. The attraction has less to do with food and cheer, though, than with the tragedies reputed to have occurred in these places long ago. Here the cruel misery of unresolved life circumstances plays on, trapping its victims in an eternity of sorrow over lost lives and loves. Some psychics say there is a darker side to hauntings in bars. They believe drinking establishments are frequented by the malicious ghosts of the addicted, who lie in wait for patrons to become inebriated and then take them on a joy ride, so to speak, to fulfill their own addictions.

Benchwarmer Bob's

Bob Lurtsema has never doubted the rumors that his restaurant, Benchwarmer Bob's Sports Cafe, stands on an ancient American Indian burial ground. After all, it is the only reasonable explanation for all the odd happenings there.

"On two separate occasions I have had American Indians come out and they explained things about burial grounds," Lurtsema says. "They said if you make peace with them [the spirits] and put something up to show that you believe, they won't bother you any more. That's why I've hung a dream catcher above the entrance."

Lurtsema isn't the only one to suspect the former nightclub is haunted. The building has changed hands seven times over the course of 30 years. The Burnsville Police Department has regularly visited the cavernous property to investigate late-night incidents called in by frightened staff tidying up after close. And servers have complained that minutes after putting all the chairs up on the bar, two would be found back on the floor facing each other as if a couple were engaged in conversation.

In the basement, a fully set table for two has been found after everything was cleaned up and put away. As well, elevators void of human passengers would mysteriously activate and travel up and down for minutes at a time.

Lurtsema's own ghostly encounter occurred during the middle of the day while he was at the front counter telling some new servers about the restaurant's hauntings.

"As I'm telling the story, the lights started to dim, then went up again. Thinking it was a staff member playing a joke, I said, 'All right, who is messing with me now.' I turned to look at the DJ booth where all the light switches are, and nobody is in there. Then the lights dimmed and went up again. For me to be telling them about the story and for that to happen was pretty eerie," he says.

Another spooky incident involved a light fixture in the basement. Lurtsema recalls being downstairs with some employees when the old fixture, earlier declared non-repairable by an electrician, suddenly turned on and began emitting a strange orange glow. The encounter made the hair on the back of his neck stand up, he says.

Though stories of unexplained phenomena at the site go back years, Lurtsema says the hauntings have quieted down some since he took the advice of his American Indian visitors and hung up the dream catcher.

Reiterating that he was told to put up something to indicate his belief in the spirits, Lurtsema says that since he hung up the dream catcher, "business has been good."

Saloon Spooks

Patrons of nightclubs often have problems with spirits, and not just the drinking kind. Ghosts haunting bars can be downright territorial, creating misery for everyone in the place—even, in some instances, long after the place is gone.

Such was the case in Lakefield, where a woman got more than she bargained for when she built her house on the site of an abandoned, long-defunct pub. Strange, unexplained events began to happen in the woman's home shortly after she moved in. A mean-spirited phantom demon began tormenting her dog. The pet became a wretched bundle of nerves and eventually required medication.

Minneapolis intuitive Jean Kellet identified the invisible tormentor as a spirit that had hung around the nightclub—

a regular, so to speak—who was evidently annoyed at the change in venue.

The First Avenue Nightclub in Minneapolis is also said to be haunted. That nightclub is housed in a former Greyhound bus station that was built on the site of old livestock corrals, where sheep and cattle were sold for slaughter. Today, ghostly sounds of bleating farm animals are heard coming from the basement, and a young woman who committed suicide at the bus station in the 1960s makes her presence felt.

Employees and patrons alike have reported strange sounds, drafts of chilly air and fleeting sightings of a woman who has long blond hair and is wearing a green army jacket and bell-bottoms. Photographs taken inside the popular club by ghost busters have shown orbs of light.

Kellet says bars are often haunted by spirits, particularly by spirits of people who had addiction problems in life. She says this happens so frequently that she can't cross the threshold of most drinking establishments without being overwhelmed by the sheer number of nasty spirits loitering about. Most of these spirits are violent, so entrenched in the addictions cycle that they just wait to prey on the weak and the vulnerable, she says.

"People who drink alcohol and then say the next day that they don't remember what they did, it's the spirits going for a ride and fulfilling their addictions that way," she says. "People with DTs when they have hallucinations are seeing things from the lower astral plane, some pretty terrifying things, and I have no doubt that they are seeing them."

Eatery Apparitions

More often than not, employees of D.B. Searle's Restaurant return to the popular St. Cloud eatery to find some portion of their previous evening's work undone.

"[Staff members] have come in and found the chairs turned backwards to the table," says manager Tom Emer, who has owned the place for the past three years. "[They've] also [told me of] cases where the elevator has gone up when no one else is in the building."

D.B. Searle's has long been haunted. It's not unusual for customers to report feeling a sudden swoosh of cold air rush past them as they dine, or to alert staff when the heavy stained glass lampshade suspended over their table begins to sway violently as if some invisible force is pushing it back and forth. Some diners have even reported feeling phantom fingers touch them.

Built in 1886, the D.B. Searle's building is one of the oldest in St. Cloud. The handsome brick structure has housed many businesses, including Colbert's Funeral Home, which operated between 1940 and the late 1960s.

The building was named for Dolson Bush Searle, an attorney and judge who came to St. Cloud in 1871. Although Searle never actually lived in the building, choosing instead to live on Second Street South, many people speculate that it is his ghost that is responsible for the haunting. Others say it is the spirit of a little boy.

Whoever the ghost is, it makes itself known to employees and clients alike. Several years ago, a server got the shock of her life when she felt a hand or fingers push down the top of her hair, which she had worn puffy that day, as she sat facing six bartenders during a training session. The waitress looked behind her to see who was playing with her hair, but no one was there. When she turned back around, the horrified look on the bartenders' faces told her that she hadn't been the only witness to the unusual event.

The ghost also teased a server late one night after closing. One of the most important closing procedures in the restaurant is the extinguishing of all table candles, which the server did before locking up for the night. Once outside on the front street the server took one last look at the dining area of the building. Instead of seeing total darkness, however, he saw a solitary candle burning in one section of the dining room. He went back into the restaurant and found the candle burning brightly, although it had been completely extinguished when he left.

Incidents like this have resulted in some of the more superstitious staff members refusing to be alone in the restaurant at night. Emer, however, says he's never personally experienced anything unusual since he's been there. Then again, that depends on how one defines unusual.

"I [used to work at] Forepaugh's Restaurant," says Emer, referring to one of St. Paul's most haunted restaurants, "so ghosts don't scare me."

Fine Dining Ghosts

One of the finest dining experiences to be had in St. Paul can be found downtown at the elegant and historic Victorian mansion known as Forepaugh's Restaurant. But one of the spookiest hauntings can be encountered there, too, if the ghosts of the original homeowner, Joseph Forepaugh, and his ill-fated lover, Molly the maid, make themselves known to guests.

Joseph Lybrandt Forepaugh was a respected pioneer, a successful entrepreneur and the senior partner of the largest wholesale dry goods house in the Midwest. When he was just 36, the world was his oyster. Forepaugh built the showpiece mansion in 1870 for his wife, Mary, and their two daughters. Spread over five lots and designed so that every window offered a splendid view of sculpted grounds and manicured gardens, the house was spectacular in its day.

Staff at this elegant restaurant are kept busy not only with regular customers but also with resident spirits.

Unfortunately, Forepaugh was dogged by an irrational fear about his wealth and obsessed needlessly over his financial affairs. His obsession became so great that in 1892, at the age of 58, Forepaugh killed himself. His crumpled body was found beside a pond with a bullet wound in his head and a revolver clutched in his hand.

News reports of the day blamed Forepaugh's death on depression. But word of an illicit love affair broke when Molly, Forepaugh's young and fetching housemaid, killed herself upon learning of her master's death. She was found hanging from a ceiling fixture in what was then a third-floor bedroom.

Servant gossip claimed Mrs. Forepaugh had caught her husband making love to Molly and forbade him to ever see her again. They say the thought of breaking off the affair sent Forepaugh spiraling into a deep despair that eventually claimed him. Prospects were looking none too good for Molly, either, being pregnant with Forepaugh's child and having just lost both her lover and her job.

Tongues really started wagging when it was revealed that Forepaugh's financial affairs were indeed in good order at the time of his death. The value of his estate was pegged at $500,000, a princely sum in 1892.

The mansion traded hands many times after Forepaugh's death and eventually fell into disrepair. The present owners purchased it in 1974, whereupon it entered its current state as the home of fine French cuisine. It is in this restaurant that serving staff report unusual things occurring, such as lights going on and off, strange sounds arising and cold spots emerging. These happenings are most common in a third-floor dining room, the former bedroom where Molly hanged herself.

Some actually claim to have seen Molly's ghost in various parts of the house. The apparition is said to resemble a very pretty dark-haired girl seen in a photograph taken during a garden party at the Forepaugh estate. The old photo hangs on the wall between the first and second floors of the restaurant. The girl, who appears to be looking at someone just outside of the frame with great adoration, is thought to be Molly.

Longtime servers at Forepaugh's say Molly is a bit of a prankster. An example of her antics occurred one night when a server named Henry was closing up the restaurant. He turned off all the lights in the building, locked the doors and walked to his car. As he reached his car, he turned to take one last look at the house. He noticed a flickering light coming from the infamous third-floor dining room.

Thinking he must have left a candle burning on one of the tables, Henry went back inside the restaurant and up the stairs to the room. When he got there, however, the room was totally dark. Henry shrugged the incident off and left the house a second time. Again he took a quick look at the restaurant when he reached his car. The light was flickering in the same window.

Henry went back inside the house and climbed the stairs once more. This time there was a candle burning brightly on the table. He said, "Molly, I'm tired and I want to go home. No more games." He then blew out the candle, left the restaurant and walked back to his car. He looked back at the restaurant. No candle was burning.

Molly is also known to wander through the dining rooms during large parties. During a special 19th-century costume event at the restaurant, an unknown woman wearing authentic period clothing glided past a server, walked down a hallway and vanished.

Forepaugh's ghost has also been seen striding proudly through his house, and it appears he is up to some of his old tricks. Evidence of his spirit was captured in a photograph taken at a wedding party at the restaurant. The photograph clearly shows a ghostly hand reaching towards the bride's knee. It is believed the hand belongs to Forepaugh, as he was reputed to have had many an illicit affair.

Alas, this photograph was stolen from its spot on the wall some time ago and hasn't been returned, leading some to believe the incriminating picture may have been removed by ghostly hands fearing retribution.

Authorial Apparition?

Few have seen the ghost that haunts the Palmer House Hotel and Restaurant in Sauk Centre. But plenty have heard it.

Those who have witnessed the ghost have reported seeing a heavy fog floating down the hallway and a vaporous cloud hovering between rooms 12 and 13. Those who have heard it have fallen victim to its late-night hijinks.

The pranks usually begin around 3 AM when the ghost is said to start roaming the hallways. Some guests report being awakened from their sleep by the sound of children whispering outside their door.

The ghost has been blamed for locking people in their rooms, knocking on doors in the middle of the night and moving heavy furniture around. It's also been charged with playing nasty tricks, such as soaking clothing (evidently with water) while the clothing's still packed away in a locked suitcase or saturating the middle of the bed while the sheets and blankets remain mysteriously dry.

The identity of the Palmer House Hotel ghost has never been established, partly because there are so many possibilities. Built in 1901 by R.L. Palmer, the hotel was primarily used by traveling salesmen. It also attracted its fair share of artists, actors, musicians and eccentrics, including one individual who reportedly committed suicide on the premises.

The building fell into a state of disrepair in the mid-1920s and remained derelict for some time. Eventually it was restored to its former glory, and it now operates as a historic inn, attracting visitors from far and wide. Most come to Sauk Centre to see its Main Street, which was immortalized in the American classic novel bearing the same name written by Nobel Prize–winning author Sinclair Lewis.

Indeed some think the ghost that haunts the Palmer House Hotel is that of Sinclair Lewis, who derived much pleasure from taunting the citizens of the town. Lewis was born in Sauk Centre and was at odds with the city almost from the moment he arrived. A loner, an introvert and an atheist in the middle of the Bible Belt, Lewis was not well accepted by the locals.

During the summer of 1902, before going off to Yale, Lewis worked at the hotel as a night clerk. Legend has it that he was fired for failing to awaken a salesman in time for him to catch the 5:30 AM train out of town.

More strain was put on the relationship between Lewis and his hometown in 1920 when *Main Street* was published. The text criticized the provincialism and bigotry of a fictitious Minnesota town called Gopher Prairie, which bore an uncanny resemblance to Sauk Centre and its residents.

Lewis wrote: "Though Gopher Prairie regards itself as a part of the Great World, compares itself to Rome and Vienna, it will not acquire the scientific spirit, the international mind, which would make it great…Its conception of a community ideal is not the grand manner, the noble aspiration, the fine aristocratic pride, but cheap labor for the kitchen and rapid increase in the price of land."

The book was an instant success. More than 180,000 copies were sold in the first six months of 1921. Today that figure is in the millions. But in Sauk Centre it caused an uproar, and in outlying areas it was banned outright. The editor of the Sauk Centre newspaper refused to acknowledge the book for several months. When he finally did comment on *Main Street*, he noted dryly that "a perusal of the book makes it possible for one to picture in his mind's eyes local characters having been injected bodily into the story."

Lewis may have made Sauk Centre into a laughingstock, but Sauk Centre had the last laugh. When the notorious author died of a heart attack in Rome in 1951, his body was cremated and his ashes flown to the United States in an urn. A funeral service was held, and afterwards Lewis's brother, Claude, decided against putting the handsome urn into the ground.

The story goes that he pried it open instead, and bent over to shake the ashes out into the waiting hole in the ground. Unfortunately, at that very moment a sizable gust of wind hit, scattering a good portion of Lewis's ashes across the cemetery.

A New Roommate

Guests booking into haunted hotels can usually count on unexplained events occurring during the course of their stay—not after they leave. But as a family of Canadian tourists discovered, there is no such thing as "just passing through" at a certain hotel in Roseville. Indeed it seems a mischievous spirit may have followed them home.

The incident occurred in 2001 as the family from Winnipeg, Manitoba, was visiting the Como Lake area of St. Paul. "Weird things kept happening to me in the hotel," confesses the mother of the family who, like many struggling to make sense of their first encounter from the great beyond, could only describe the incidents as bizarre. "I have always believed in supernatural experiences, but I never thought that one would happen to me," she says.

The unusual events began in the hotel room the morning after the family checked in when a pair of pajama bottoms seemingly vanished. "I remembered that in the morning I had folded them and put them on top of one of the suitcases," the mother says. "The pajama top was where I had left it, but the bottoms were nowhere to be found.

"We emptied both suitcases and checked the bathroom. Not there. We remade the beds and shook out all of the bed linens in the process. Nothing. The girls decided they would ask the evening housekeeper if she could check the hotel's laundry area. As they left, I decided to check the bathroom again, but found nothing.

"I walked past one of the beds and as I was doing this I was looking at the floor. Once past the bed I turned around and there they were, lying neatly folded on the floor in the spot that I had just walked over."

In a separate encounter in the bathroom, the mother had just pulled a tissue from the holder and began blowing her nose. "I was looking down into the sink as I did this, so I know the sink was definitely empty," she says. "I turned around to put the tissue in the garbage. As I looked back into the sink, there was a new tissue neatly spread out in the sink. I have no idea as to how it could have gotten there."

But perhaps the most nerve-wracking encounter occurred as the mother was packing her suitcase to go home.

"I was looking for a piece of underwear. I held the black bra in my hands and I remember thinking, *I'm sure I left this bra at home*. I searched the suitcase for the matching panty. I could not find it anywhere, so I notified housekeeping that I had lost this article of clothing," she says. "I know that I packed the bra back into the suitcase with the rest of my underwear. When I got home I opened my special underwear drawer to put away some of the underwear that I had not worn. Sitting there folded in the top of the drawer was the black bra and panties.

"Go figure."

4
Ghosts
in
Public

～

Few people will ever see a spirit appear in human form but plenty will experience other phenomena of the hereafter. Footsteps hurrying down empty hallways, laughter coming from no obvious source and phantom furniture being moved in empty rooms are all good indicators that spirits are at play. Sightings are fleeting and often manifest where traumatic events have occurred, their gruesome details often disconcerting to those who happen to witness them. Other spirits are so lifelike in appearance that they may not be noticed, except for their distinctive old-fashioned style of dress. These are the spirits that cleaning staff or security guards see late at night and, mistaking them for flesh-and-blood thieves, chase—a fruitless endeavor if there ever was one.

～

79 East Second Street

Several historic buildings in Winona lay claim to being haunted—and with good reason. Take the building at 79 East Second Street, for instance. Although it is currently occupied by Pieces of the Past, a furniture, gift and upholstery store, it has a checkered history that is certainly conducive to ghosts.

This particular building was built in the late 1850s and was the only structure to survive a fire that wiped out downtown Winona in the 1860s. It housed a variety of businesses over the years, with perhaps the most intriguing combination being that of a law office on the ground floor and a brothel on the top two floors.

According to Walter Bennick, archivist at the Winona County Historical Society, the building was home to Artz Brothers (Robert & Alex) Sample Rooms, Wine, Liquors, Cigars between 1890 and 1898. By 1898 that business had not only undergone a name change—to Alex A Artz Sample Rooms, Wines, Liquors, Cigars—it had an extra product line: a number of single women who were referred to as "ladies of the night."

"There was a train station across the street from the address, so the 'ladies of the night' seemed reasonable," Bennick says.

Many of the building's ghost stories are tied to these wild times. For example, it is said that a prostitute was shot and killed on the building's original staircase. And though that particular staircase no longer exists, the overwhelming scent of cheap perfume occasionally manifests itself in the area where it once stood, leaving some to believe the woman's spirit never left the spot where she died.

In 1905, the Winona Candy Company moved into the building. Then, in 1930, the candy company added a warehouse at the back for the Winona Radiator and Sheet Metal Company. The two coexisted on the property until 1933 when Cal's Auto Body Service occupied the space.

In 1936, the building became home to its longest tenant, the Sunshine Café. Then, between the 1960s and 1988, it housed the Sunshine Bar & Café. During that time, the large apartments upstairs acted as a communal haven for hippies of the free-love generation. After that, the building sat vacant for two years until the opening of Banger's Pub, a local watering hole said to be haunted by so many ghosts it was impossible to count them all.

Some spirits were easily detected, like the habitual pool player who came out after closing time to shoot a ghostly game or two. Other phenomena were more mysterious, such as light bulbs that glowed from yellow to orange, a phantom cat that mewed and a jukebox that played songs long after it was unplugged. Then there were the unexplained noises, described as sounding very much like someone throwing heavy pieces of furniture around otherwise empty rooms.

How long the building has been haunted is anyone's guess. What is known is that the first documented haunting occurred in 1988, when the building underwent an extensive renovation. Michelle Olson, owner of the building at the time, told the *Winona Post* that strange noises would start up at night that didn't have anything to do with the remodeling.

"They were extremely loud noises, too—it sounded like someone was tearing the place apart. It sounded like things were being thrown from the ceiling to the floor, and all of us who were there heard them," she is quoted as saying. "It was to the point that we called the police...we thought there was an intruder in the building, [but] we never found anything. It would be quiet while the police were there and then it would start again when they left."

Another ghost, believed to be a male, was heard on an almost daily basis running up and down the stairs in the wee hours of the morning. He was nicknamed "the runner," and his hurried footsteps were loud enough to wake staff members living upstairs. When the harried employees came downstairs, however, they found nothing but an empty pub.

One such employee claimed this ghost had repeatedly appeared in his room at night. The employee said he would wake up to find a tall, hazy white figure standing at the foot of his bed, and somehow he knew it was a man.

At least two former bartenders said the building's ghosts frequently moved things in the basement. One bartender claimed to have actually witnessed something move while he was there alone. "He ran upstairs right away and wouldn't go down there again," Olson told the *Post*.

Banger's Pub closed up shop in 1995. The building was then opened as Jake's Saloon and has operated rather uneventfully ever since. In fact, Duane Peterson, who in 2000 opened Pieces of the Past along with his wife, Cheri, says the building's haunted reputation is news to him. "I'm not aware of the hauntings," he says. "Even the last guy that owned it as a bar, he came in, never mentioned anything about ghosts."

Peterson says the tenants renting the five-bedroom apartment upstairs haven't complained of ghosts, either. He also says he's never had anything terribly unusual happen in the building late at night, even though he's often working at that time. "But," he adds, "I'm going to start looking now."

Wabasha Street Caves

On some nights, when the conditions are right, visitors to the Wabasha Street Caves just might hear the distant echo of big band music, laughter and clinking glasses. Or they might witness doors opening and closing on their own, lights turning on and off and spirits ranging from the benign to the malevolent cavorting about.

The Wabasha Street Caves, which extend about 150 feet into the bluffs below the street that bears their name, were mined in 1840, and their fine rock and silica sand were used to build some of the first roads in St. Paul. The depth of the tunnels meant the caves stayed cool year-round. In fact, once the caves were depleted of their sands, they were used as a cold storage area for perishable food items.

The interesting eco-climate of the caves also came into play in the mid-1880s, when they underwent yet another creative transformation at the hands of a group of French immigrants. Louis Lambert, Charles Etienne and Albert Mouchenott established a mushroom farm inside the caves, a business that remained lucrative for years.

Eventually, the property was passed along to Mouchenott's daughter, Josephine Lehmann. Unfortunately, Lehmann seemed to prefer gangsters to mushrooms. By the time the Roaring Twenties rolled around, and at the height of Prohibition, Lehmann had converted the caves into a bar, priming her guests with illegal booze, including moonshine and bathtub gin.

The place was such a hit that in the 1930s it was developed into a notorious speakeasy. Lehmann spared no expense as she renovated the once-dowdy caves into a lavish nightclub called the Castle Royal. Lehman and her husband,

William, went to town, turning parts of the caves into curved rooms with domed ceilings, and furnishing them with lavish fireplaces, marble fountains, a 50-foot long bar and a 1600-square-foot dance floor.

When the Castle Royal opened on October 26, 1933, it was granted the first post-Prohibition liquor licence—issued six months before Prohibition ended. While city officials and policemen turned a blind eye, the Castle Royal quickly became a favorite haunt of and safe haven for big name gangsters, including John Dillinger and Ma Barker and her boys. It is this lively era—one of gunfights, rub outs, bootleg liquor and girls—that most of the ghost stories come from.

Deborah Frethem, who runs tours of the Wabasha Street Caves through Down in History Tours Inc., has seen evidence of ghostly goings-on. In July 1998 Frethem was taking a tourist through the unfinished back part of the caves, which at the time were in near-original condition. The client, who had been taking pictures, ran out of film, which was unfortunate considering what happened next.

"I looked up and saw a strange mist," Frethem says. "My client saw the same thing. We were so scared we grabbed onto each other's arms." The frightened pair watched as the mist developed into a vaguely human shape, with the head and shoulders clearly formed. "It was very indistinct," Frethem says. "It wasn't like I saw a man but I knew instinctively that it was a man."

The figure started to move towards Frethem and her client, who were still huddled together in fright. "It walked right through us, and as it did I'm certain the temperature dropped by 10 degrees," Frethem says, adding that she was overwhelmed by a sense of evil so powerful that she feared for her life. "I was overcome by such a feeling of malevolence.

He wanted us out of there. He wanted to hurt us so badly, but for some reason was powerless to do so. I sensed that if he could have hurt us, he would have."

Frethem says one of the first and perhaps most famous ghost stories to come out of the caves occurred in 1934. It began when a scullery maid was tidying up after closing time. As she went about her rounds, she stumbled across four men drinking and arguing in a back room. Scared because the men appeared to be gangsters, the maid went nervously about her duties, listening to their conversation as it became more and more belligerent.

The arguing came to a head at around 4 AM with the sound of semiautomatic gunfire. The maid ran into the room. There she found three bullet-riddled bodies lying on the floor in pools of blood. Tables were overturned and chairs were strewn about as if a brawl had preceded the gunfire.

Frightened out of her wits, the maid called the police. When they arrived 90 minutes later, however, they did not find bodies or blood, just a room with tables and chairs covered in crisp white linen tablecloths. They searched the fireplace but found nothing out of place there either. So they left, thinking the maid had been drinking and had lost all her senses.

Later, as the maid was trying to figure out what happened, she came across bullet holes in the stone fireplace. They'd been there for some time, reportedly the result of an earlier rub out. According to Frethem, three men, undoubtedly gangsters, are believed to be buried under a cement floor in one of the unfinished caves. Could it be the ghosts of these men that the maid saw?

The next reported spooky encounter in the Wabasha Street Caves occurred decades later. Like many other businesses during the Dirty Thirties, Castle Royal fell victim to the

Great Depression and eventually closed. The caves sat vacant until 1977, when they underwent another transformation, this time into a disco.

Frethem says the encounter in this disco involved a waiter who was carrying a tray of glasses into one of the back caves to set up for the evening. In the cave stood a man wearing a pinstriped suit with white lapels, white shoes and a white Panama hat. The startled waiter asked the man if he needed any help, at which point the figure glared at him and walked right through the wall.

The caves changed hands many times until the early 1990s, when they settled into their current ownership and became a tourist attraction. Luckily for sightseers, not all the ghosts at Down in History Tours Inc. are hostile, Frethem says. For example, there is a friendly ghost in the caves that often pours her a drink.

"[One night] I was drinking a glass of wine and went into the office to change out of my costume," she says. "When I came back my wine glass was full. I thanked the bartender, but he denied having filled my glass.

"[Another] night I was bartending and worked until closing. My husband and I locked up and had a glass of wine while we were cleaning up. I set the empty glass on the counter. My husband went outside to throw out the trash, so I was alone in the cave. I turned around to put the evening's receipts into the cash bag. When I turned back around, my wine glass was full."

A spookier ghostly encounter occurred during a private party of about 300 guests. Frethem was costumed as a late 1800s madam named Nina Clifford. While she was working the room she saw another woman in a similar period costume.

The event, however, was not a costume party. The woman walked up to her and then disappeared right through a wall.

Frethem says she has had many more ghostly encounters while working at the caves. But by far the scariest occurred when she was there as a patron socializing with friends. "I was sitting on a barstool talking…when I felt a cold, clammy hand grab my left shoulder," she says. "I could feel the fingers and thumb and it grabbed me so hard that it spun me around."

Frethem looked to see who was holding her shoulder but no one was there, much to the astonishment of everyone present. "Needless to say I didn't tell any more ghost stories that night."

Soldier Spirits

Ghosts of Civil War soldiers are said to walk the area of the former site of historic Fort Ripley, now located within the boundaries of Camp Ripley near Little Falls.

Sandy Erickson, administrator of the Minnesota Military Museum, says people have been reporting these ghosts for years and she's even heard of one recent sighting.

"My husband told me that during summer annual training someone told him that [he was] driving…along the road near the old fort site around dusk and that he saw at least one man and possibly more walking alongside the road dressed in a Civil War–type uniform and he thought they were Civil War re-enactors," she says.

"He thought it was odd that they would be out there with training actively going on in the area. When he looked back in his rearview mirror again to make sure he had seen correctly, they were gone."

Revenge from the Hereafter

Revenge is a powerful emotion in life, but at Saint Mary's University of Minnesota in Winona, it has proven to be even more formidable in death.

In 1995, Saint Mary's College was renamed Saint Mary's University of Minnesota. Since 1943, students living on the third story of the Heffron Hall Dormitory have reported being awakened at night by the sound of footsteps and the tapping of a cane in the hallways. Unexplained cold winds have been felt in the corridor. Notices on bulletin boards have flapped as if moved by a stiff breeze, though no breeze exists. And more than one student has been prevented from entering the floor by some sort of invisible force.

In 1989, *USA Today* deemed the Heffron Hall Dormitory "Minnesota's Most Legendary Haunted Place." The story of the haunting at Saint Mary's University goes back to 1915, when a crazed priest named Father Laurence Michael Lesches shot a bishop in cold blood in a twisted act of revenge.

On August 27, 1915, Patrick Heffron, bishop of the Winona diocese, was celebrating morning mass alone in a small chapel on the fourth floor of Saint Mary's Hall when he heard footsteps hastily enter the place of worship and stop. Bishop Heffron turned to see his nemesis, Father Laurence Michael Lesches, standing behind him with a gun in his hand. Bishop Heffron watched in horror as Lesches pointed the Smith & Wesson revolver at him and pulled the trigger three times, hitting him twice. Shock, pain and disbelief spilled across Bishop Heffron's face as he crumpled to the ground. Lesches fled the church.

The badly injured bishop dragged himself across the floor before collapsing in a bloody heap at the chapel entrance. He was discovered moments later by Father Thomas Narmoyle, who saw Lesches flee as he rushed over to the chapel to investigate the sound of gunfire. Bishop Heffron was whisked away to the hospital. When police arrived six minutes later, they acted on Father Narmoyle's eyewitness account and began the search for Lesches.

They didn't have to look very far. Police located Lesches in his room, pistol in hand. He was acting nervously and did not deny the shooting. In fact, he said he shot Bishop Heffron because the bishop had denied him his own parish, declaring him unfit for religious life and better suited to farm life. Lesches was arrested without incident and later charged with assault in the first degree.

At the hospital, police questioned Bishop Heffron about his relationship with Lesches. The two had known each other for nearly 20 years but they had never been friends. Bishop Heffron described Lesches as unstable, arrogant, abrasive, self-absorbed and hotheaded—a man with little tact and few friends.

The bishop, however, was no angel himself. It was true he had single-handedly raised the funds to establish Saint Mary's College, but he was also a domineering perfectionist who lived his life by exacting standards. And colleagues like Lesches who did not meet those same expectations bore the full brunt of his wrath.

Bishop Heffron was known to beat or shun those who did not follow his orders. He was famous for setting people up for failure by promoting them to important positions beyond their grasp simply to prove their incompetence. He held others down in menial positions to damage their pride.

This savage streak had been sufficient grounds for his dismissal from his previous position at the St. Paul Cathedral in 1896. But at Saint Mary's College the bishop was free to do as he pleased.

Days before the shooting, Bishop Heffron had again turned down Lesches's request for his own diocese, saying he was too unstable for such a responsibility. Lesches, now 55 and desperate, did not take the refusal quietly. He begged Bishop Heffron to change his mind. But the bishop refused, saying he would not "under any circumstances" put Lesches in charge of a parish. He then suggested Lesches "consider farm work, which would not require close personal relationships."

After the meeting with Heffron, Lesches returned to Saint Mary's Hall. There he had an eerie encounter with Father Bernard Kramer, an assistant at St. Joseph's Church in Winona. In his book, *Gathering a People*, William Crozier describes the encounter: "That evening the priests were in the common room; some of them were playing cards. Father Lesches paced back and forth, muttering the damn bishop this and the damn bishop that. Turning to Kramer, who was playing bridge, Lesches said: 'What would you do, Bernie, if the bishop refused you an appointment?' Intent on the game and probably annoyed at the pacing priest, Kramer replied, 'I'd shoot the ———!' "

Once recovered sufficiently from his wounds, Bishop Heffron was able to testify against Lesches at the trial. During his testimony, the bishop described Lesches as unstable in his work. He said Lesches was incapable of settling down in one place, and was a burden who always seemed a day away from hunger and homelessness.

Bishop Heffron mentioned the argument that preceded the shooting. "I told him that he was too emotionally unstable to handle such an assignment," he is quoted as testifying. "I had believed that for years, and again I suggested that he consider farm work, which would not require close, personal relationships."

Bishop Heffron testified that he believed Lesches was not able to distinguish between right and wrong at the moment of the shooting, nor was he able to make sense of the repercussions. Chief of Police George Huck testified that Lesches confessed he shot the bishop because he was upset over his remarks about Lesches's soul being no good and because he had suggested that Lesches belonged on a farm.

After only two days, Lesches was acquitted of the assault charge on the grounds of insanity. Judge George Granger sentenced him to treatment at the State Hospital for the Dangerously Insane in St. Peter, Minnesota, on December 3, 1915.

Once Lesches was locked up, life went on productively for Bishop Heffron. Before he died on November 23, 1927, he established 27 churches, helped set up St. Mary's Hospital in Rochester, and had a new dormitory on the Saint Mary's campus christened in his honor.

Lesches, meanwhile, was left to languish in the mental hospital. Until 1931, that is, when, after cooperating with doctors and undergoing treatments for paranoia, he was finally pronounced to be in sound mental health. At that time, Lesches was still under the guardianship of the Winona diocese, so he wrote the parish asking for permission to be discharged. Bishop Heffron's successor, Bishop Francis Relly, however, refused to sign the necessary papers to have him released.

Were Lesches not clinically mad before, the cruelty of this decision certainly would have put him over the edge. Indeed,

1931 marked the beginning of a series of disturbing incidents at Saint Mary's College that were attributed to the mad priest as he languished in the asylum.

In May, just after Lesches was denied release from the hospital, a nun entered the third-floor room of Rev. Edward W. Lynch in Heffron Hall. Father Lynch and Lesches had been neighbors, and their relationship was one of bitter feuds and heated arguments. On that spring morning, a nun found Father Lynch sprawled dead across his bed. His body was charred beyond recognition, but the sheets underneath him were untouched and nothing else in the room was burned or even singed.

Father Lynch's Bible was also scorched, save for a single passage. "And the Lord shall come at the sound of the trumpets," it read, the very words Lesches is said to have shouted to Lynch many times during heated arguments.

According to the May 15, 1931, edition of the *Winona Republican-Herald*, Father Lynch died from an electrical shock. The front-page article said the freak accident occurred when he reached over to shut off a reading lamp attached to his metal headboard and accidentally touched a steam radiator at the same time. Winona County coroner P.A. Mattison determined that the lamp was the source of the current that sent the fatal surge of electricity coursing through Father Lynch's body.

But the logic of Mattison's official cause of death left a lot to be desired. Records of the Mississippi Valley Power & Light Company showed that the lamp fed off a charge of 110 volts. And experts said that was simply not enough juice to kill someone, never mind char a body beyond recognition.

Many blamed the strange death on Lesches. Although he was locked away at the hospital in St. Peter, he was accused of putting some sort of vengeful curse on Father Lynch. He was credited with the power to direct deadly thoughts towards people he hated from within the confines of the asylum. This rumor grew when another priest from Saint Mary's died in a fire, and three more were killed in a fiery airplane crash that same year.

On January 10, 1943, after 29 years in the mental home, Lesches died. The legendary haunting of Heffron Hall began after his death.

The first eerie occurrence took place in 1945 when the facility was a dorm for seminary students. Seminarian Mike O'Malley was up late at night when he heard someone walking up and down the hall. The footsteps stopped suddenly outside his room and were followed by a knock on his door. O'Malley opened the door and found a cloaked figure standing there in stony silence, his face shrouded in the shadow of his hood. Thinking it one of the priests, O'Malley asked, "What do you want, Father?"

The figure reportedly let out a deep, garbled, otherworldly moan. A startled O'Malley repeated his question: "What do you want, Father?" The answer gave O'Malley the fright of his life. "I...want...YOU," the figure moaned. Upset and a little frightened, O'Malley wound up and punched the figure in the face, breaking his hand in the process.

The commotion woke O'Malley's roommate, who stumbled out of bed and turned on the light to see what was going on. It is said he caught a glimpse of the stranger's face, which he later described as having a clay-like complexion.

Disciplinary records from that day reveal that a student broke his hand in a fight in the cafeteria. There was, however, no report anywhere on campus of someone with a broken jaw.

Another bizarre incident is said to have happened at Heffron Hall a short time later. Legend has it that one of the students who lived there had the unique talent of putting himself into a trance and communicating with spirits. One evening after coming out of such a trance the normally cheerful student appeared to be agitated and anxious.

And his agitation was not unfounded. For the strange feeling was followed by an even stranger incident a short time later. After finishing up in the bathroom, the young man flushed the urinal and immediately saw a thick red, blood-like fluid running down the opposite urinal.

Wanting to get out of there, he ran to the sink to wash his hands. When he turned on the taps, however, the same thick blood red fluid poured from the faucet. He ran out of the washroom and down the hall. He heard the door close behind him, then reopen and close again. Then he heard footsteps following him. He looked over his shoulder and saw no one, but the footsteps continued. So he headed to his neighbor's room. Unfortunately, his friend did not believe his story in the slightest.

That was the last time the young man was seen alive. Soon after, his body was found sprawled across his bed, his face twisted in a grimace of agonized terror, the impression of a cross burned onto his chest.

Stories of hauntings at Heffron Hall continued to circulate for years. Finally, in 1969, staff members of the college's monthly student publication undertook a scientific investigation into the strange happenings. A team of photographers, researchers and witnesses established an inventory of the happenings and then attempted to verify them. The team spent two nights on the third floor of the dormitory, using all kinds of sophisticated ghost-detecting equipment.

The group detected consistent, drastic drops in temperature in the long corridor each evening at precisely 1:45 AM, about the same time Lesches was known to have died. These temperature changes were not consistent throughout the hall but instead confined to a few cold spots. Drafts from windows and doors and other usual causes were ruled out as being responsible.

The temperature change was recorded traveling down the hallway from east to west at a rate of 100 feet every 30 seconds. Cameras taking pictures during the sudden drop in temperature showed blurred areas, which were believed to indicate a change of pressure.

The ghost of a vengeful priest haunts Saint Mary's University.

While the study was deemed inconclusive, many students at Saint Mary's have formed their own opinions of the unusual experiences at the facility. They believe the ghost of Father Lesches still roams the hall. After all, Father Lesches *is* buried in the St. Mary's Cemetery close to the campus.

Haunting the State Fair

Many ghosts are said to haunt the Minnesota State Fairgrounds, including one in the form of a little brown bird. This feathered creature, referred to as Wayne, has made a pilgrimage to the fair every year since 1986, arriving on opening day and settling in near the historic Ye Old Mill ride.

The bird's species has yet to be identified, but some operators of the popular tunnel-of-love-style ride believe the funny-looking flyer is actually a reincarnation of Wayne Murray, a long-time ride maintenance operator. Wayne died in 1986, the same year the strange bird started showing up at the Ye Old Mill ride.

Marna Keenan, whose husband's family built the ride in 1913, agrees that the brown bird could be the reincarnation of Wayne. "We always feel that Wayne is with us," Keenan told the *St. Paul Pioneer Press.*

The ghost of a young man with sandy-colored hair is also said to haunt the Minnesota State Fairgrounds. He's been sighted dozens of times—mostly in broad daylight—in and around the "bunker," a small building located in the infield area behind the grandstand stage.

The fair's entertainment supervisor claims he saw the spooky figure twice in 1994. One sighting occurred in a stairway leading out of the bunker, right in the middle of the afternoon. The supervisor was standing by himself on the steps when a man in his 20s or 30s suddenly appeared out of nowhere and stood next to him. The man had sandy-colored hair and a mustache. The supervisor, slightly taken aback, did a double take. When he looked back at the spot where the man had been standing, there was no one there.

Later that week, a security guard reported seeing the same man inside the bunker at night. Reportedly, the guard watched a man with sandy-colored hair walk into a room that had no exit except for the door he came in. Curious as to the man's identity, the guard walked towards the room, keeping his eyes on that door. When he entered the room, however, the man was gone, as if he had vanished into thin air.

There are other less easily identifiable ghosts at the state fair. One such specter has been spotted in the grandstand area. In 1994, during a rock concert, several witnesses saw what looked like a man sitting on the edge of the grandstand roof with his feet dangling over the side. Fearing for the man's safety, St. Paul police officers climbed up to the roof the only way possible, on a single ladder. By the time they reached the roof, the ghostly image was gone.

Over the years there have also been reports of a spectral pig that appears in the basement of the state fair's cattle barn. It's likely this story gave rise to the legend of "the pigman," a ghost thought to be half man and half swine. The pigman is said to grow more ferocious each year. Unlike the other hauntings at the state fair grounds, the pigman is purely fictional.

Looking for a Lost Lover

True love is probably the closest thing to heaven on earth that most humans will ever experience. As a result, those who've had it stolen away prematurely through death, disaster or deception often carry the anguish to their grave—and occasionally, beyond.

In Winona, an illuminated figure of a young Victorian-era woman wearing a white nightgown wanders up and down Third Street in an eternal search for her lost lover.

No one knows for certain what tragic events conspired to separate the young lady from her true love, but inhabitants of an apartment building on East Third Street have a pretty good idea where the tragedy occurred. For years tenants from different suites, and even visitors staying overnight in the building, have been plagued by a recurrent dream so vivid it has chased grown men out of their own homes.

The dream involves an attractive young woman with long auburn hair walking down an 1890s-era version of East Third Street, evidently in search of her lover. Her search takes her to a building standing where the apartments now are.

The young lady, who appears to be in her late teens, enters the building. The dreamers say they know instinctively that this is where her lover is. There is no happy reunion, however. The original building on the site is said to have housed a mortuary and later a funeral parlor. As her betrothed practiced neither profession, it is almost certain that he died an unexpected and tragic death.

The ghost of Third Street may be doomed to spend eternity reliving that initial traumatic moment of shock and heartbreak, but it's quite clear she isn't content to go it alone. Male tenants and visitors who have had the dream recall being overwhelmed by the sense that the young woman was searching for them.

But the strangest activities seem to occur on the building's second floor. Some tenants say they have actually felt a ghost touch them, running invisible fingers through their hair or stroking their arms while they watched television or snoozed on the couch. Whether or not this phantom is the forlorn lovely that wanders Third Street is a matter of opinion. Such behavior seems a little brazen for a young woman of Victorian times and sensibilities. And given the building's history, the ghost could be any number of souls, including that of another woman who died there in the 1950s.

What is clear is that there is a ghost in the building. There are unusual cold spots around the apartments and tenants say footsteps can be heard going up and down the stairs when no one is there. Previously broken clocks suddenly begin working again—even after the batteries are taken out. Smaller items, such as lighters, coins and television remote controls, disappear almost the minute they are set down, only to turn up later in the exact spot they went missing or in entirely odd places such as the bathroom or the cat litter box.

Visitors to the apartments also complain that pocket change left in a pile on a dresser is later found stacked on top of the television set or the kitchen table.

Very few tenants have witnessed these activities as they have occurred, but stunned renters did watch as a lamp fixture on a vaulted ceiling fell. That fixture did not fall straight down as was expected. Instead, it fell at an angle into a laundry basket full of clothes, which prevented it from smashing.

This unexplained phenomenon caused some tenants to pack up and move out of the building. They are now happy to report that it is much easier to find their keys.

An Endless Execution

Had the old adage of "measure twice, cut once" been applied to William Williams's execution in 1913, he probably wouldn't be haunting the staff lunchroom of St. Paul's Ramsey County Courthouse with quite so much vengeance.

As it was, Williams's horribly botched execution led to such a public outcry over the death penalty that the cold-blooded murderer entered the annals of history as the last person ever executed in the state of Minnesota.

William was convicted in the early 1900s of the sexual assault and murder of a young boy. He was sentenced to death by hanging. His executioner was young and inexperienced and, having never performed a hanging before, was not particularly well versed in the methodologies used to calculate the desired length of the hanging rope.

The lad was unaware that rope can stretch, a factor that a more experienced hangman would have tested with weights. Nor was he aware of the considerable stretching capacity of the human neck.

Many St. Paul residents came to watch Williams's execution, including the victim's grieving mother. When the platform fell away from under his feet, the rope stretched eight inches. Williams's neck stretched another four, giving just enough length for his feet to hit the floor.

The executioner and members of the public watched in horror as the condemned man dangled from the ceiling and scrabbled about the floor on his tiptoes. Finally, after about 16 minutes, the executioner ran up to Williams, grabbed him by the knees and pulled him down, breaking his neck.

The basement staff lunchroom of the Ramsey County Courthouse rests on the spot where Williams's gruesome execution took place nearly 90 years ago. To this day, people in the lunchroom say that every so often they catch a glimpse of a man dropping from the ceiling on the end of a noose as if coming from a trapdoor.

There's no question of who that man might be.

Uncanny Courthouse

Several ghosts haunt the Ramsey County Courthouse in St. Paul alongside William Williams. Some had legitimate business inside its hallowed halls while they lived. Others persist from the days when a prison stood on the grounds.

The site has been a hub of activity for more than 150 years. First it was a town square, then a jail, and finally, in 1931, it became home to the city's 19-story courthouse and city hall. The present occupant has quite a history.

Not only is the building on the site of the hangings of both the first and last persons to be executed in Minnesota, but it also sits on top of what used to be a secret underground tunnel built during the Prohibition era. And more than rum was run in those tunnels. Famous St. Paul madam Nina Clifford and her "girls" regularly used the connection between Ramsey Hill and downtown to visit the mayor's quarters.

The tunnel, discovered in 1999 during the construction of the Science Museum, also led straight to council chambers. What entertaining city hall meetings those must have been!

The Ramsey County Courthouse has been described as a monument to art-deco high-rise architecture, using both the American perpendicular and zigzag moderne art-deco styles. The interior is finished in expensive domestic and foreign woods and marbles, each floor designed with its own type of timber. The stunning black marble pillars in Memorial Hall carry the names of all the people from Ramsey County who have died in past wars, from World War I to the Grenada Conflict.

In this hall people have reported hearing mysterious chuckling and a woman's voice calling out. Misty black and white shapes have supposedly been seen in the lobby by the elevator area, as well as ghostly figures of men dressed in clothing from the 1930s and 1940s. These figures vanish when anyone approaches.

Cleaning staff in the building claim to have experienced cold chills and their hair standing up on their arms. They've reported hearing mysterious footsteps, the jangling of keys, doors creaking open and doors slamming shut when no one else is around. They also say they get the distinct impression that someone is riding in the elevator with them as they go about their rounds late at night.

Ramsey County commissioner Victoria Reinhardt says even her office has been affected by such experiences. In the 1980s Reinhardt was working as a commissioner's assistant. Shortly after she was elected, her boss died suddenly. A few weeks later, Reinhardt's assistant, Pam, was in her office working late. A cleaning lady was working in the outer office and came running into Pam's office saying she'd just seen a strange man in a trench coat enter the room.

Pam assured her that no one had come into the office but the cleaning woman insisted. She went on to describe what the man looked like. "As the cleaning lady described the person she saw, Pam said she knew who it was. It was my boss," Reinhardt says.

Some floors, especially 7 and 14, are more haunted than others and have a negative feel to them, say staffers. Police were called one night when a security guard saw a shape race up the stairs after he called out for it to stop. A dog was brought in to track down the intruder. The dog ended up going to the seventh floor but no intruder was ever found.

Another ghost, said to be dressed in 1800s-era knickers, has been seen in the elevator, apparently trying to fix the elevator, all the while chuckling to himself. A man from the early 1900s is said to be seen checking a stopwatch as he walks in and out of a wall on the first floor. And the ghost of a shoeshine man turns up from time to time.

But perhaps one of the more startling incidents occurred in the courthouse during the 1940s when a man carrying a briefcase approached a security guard on night duty. The man, wearing a double-breasted suit and looking very much like a lawyer, appeared confused, so the security guard asked what business he had at the courthouse in the middle of the night. The man looked at the guard and appeared to become even more confused. He turned on his heel and walked away abruptly, disappearing into a bluish haze right before the startled guard's eyes.

Another haunting at the courthouse has to do with lost love. Several people have reported seeing a young woman wearing a 1930s-style wedding dress pacing up and down the hallways, waiting for her intended to show for their wedding. He never does.

The hauntings in the Ramsey County Courthouse are said to have increased since the building underwent a major renovation between 1990 and 1993. More than $48 million was spent to bring the building up to code and restore it to its original splendor.

According to an article in the *St. Paul Pioneer Press*, a construction worker who was part of the crew in 1992 reported tools and lumber moving from place to place, items and equipment disappearing and miraculously turning up again and water pouring out of disconnected pipes.

Psychics have identified seven spirits active in the building but say there's nothing malevolent about any of them. It just seems as if they died and never moved on.

Indeed Reinhardt says she finds the presence of the ghosts somewhat reassuring. "I'm in my office very often late into the evening and [I] feel the presence of spirits," she says. "But I've never felt any fear. It's almost a calming feeling for me."

State Capitol Specters

Minnesota's State Capitol Building is said to be haunted by the ghost of its designer, prominent American architect Cass Gilbert.

Visitors and staff at the building report seeing an apparition in Edwardian dress in the hallways looking intently at the building's various structural features, as if inspecting the workmanship. And who could blame him? The capitol building was Gilbert's first major public work after he made his mark in the architectural world as the father of the modern skyscraper for his design of the 60-story Woolworth Building in New York.

But Gilbert isn't the only soul lingering in the State Capitol Building. An apparition of a man in regimental dress has been reported lurking about on the second floor. Because of his distinctive uniform, many believe this is the ghost of Colonel William Covill.

Colonel Covill fought with the Minnesota Regiment during the Civil War and was wounded at Gettysburg. His injuries were so severe that he was rendered an invalid, discharged and sent home.

Colonel Covill's grave illness prevented him from attending a celebration honoring him and his regiment at the State Capitol Building's dedication in 1905. Word is that missing this great tribute caused the colonel so much distress it hastened his death later in the year. The colonel received an even greater accolade in death, however. His body was the first ever to lie in state inside the rotunda.

The statue of Colonel Covill on the building's second floor gazes down at a regimental flag hanging on the first floor. It is said that if one looks closely enough, Colonel Covill's ghost can be seen beside the statue looking down into the atrium as if taking in the celebration he missed.

The ghost of architect Cass Gilbert is said to still roam the halls of Minnesota's State Capitol Building, inspecting his architectural design.

Riverview Hall Haunting

With bats in the belfry and a resident ghost wandering the corridors, Riverview Hall seems more like prime haunted house material than a national register landmark home. But as the second-oldest building on the 132-year-old St. Cloud University campus, Riverview Hall is exactly that—and more.

Designed by St. Paul architect Clarance Johnston, bosom buddy of American architect Cass Gilbert, Riverview Hall was completed in 1913 at a cost of $60,000. The massive structure, built with St. Cloud yellow brick, was designed to house the St. Cloud model school, a facility that gave student teachers a chance to practice teaching actual elementary-school–level classes.

It wasn't until the 1960s, when Riverview Hall was taken over by the university's English department, that any hint of a ghost surfaced. Professor John Bovee was working in his office one night at around 11 PM. Bovee thought he was alone in the building, so he was startled to hear the sound of a woman's high-heeled shoes coming down the hallway. He poked his head out of his office door to see if a colleague was approaching. But no one was in the hallway, and the footfalls ceased as suddenly as they had started.

A decade later, at 10:45 PM, a custodian named Judo Anderson was working on the main floor near the bottom of the grand staircase when he heard what sounded like the tapping of high-heeled shoes coming from the floor above. He listened as the footsteps made their way to the top of the staircase. He waited for someone to appear, but no one did. Instead he heard the main door open. But no one was in the doorway, either.

Bill Morgan, a columnist with the *St. Cloud Times*, has followed the Riverview Hall story for years. He says bats invade the building in the late summer and early fall. But as far as he knows, no new hauntings have been reported.

One unexplained incident did occur in 1980. It involved a grandfather clock that stood at the head of Riverview Hall's grand staircase since 1913. Teachers arriving on November 3, 1980, discovered the clock was missing.

According to a newspaper report, the clock was found intact later that night in the middle of Stearns County Road 75. Although there is no official record, some say the hands on the clock face were stuck at 11 PM.

Loon Lake Cemetery

Loon Lake Cemetery near Lakefield is said to be one of the most haunted places in Minnesota. It's also reputed to be one of the most dangerous—and with good cause.

Located a short distance from the highway between Jackson and Petersburg, Loon Lake Cemetery is the eternal resting place of three witches brutally executed more than 100 years ago. The spirits of these witches reportedly frequent the grounds, waiting to make good on their curse to deliver a most unpleasant and unnatural death to anyone who dares desecrate their graves.

Mary Jane, considered the most powerful of the three witches, was beheaded by the townspeople of Petersburg in 1881. Mary Jane's curse is taken especially seriously because she is said to have possessed highly developed supernatural powers. Legend has it that people who tread upon the grave of this witch will die within 72 hours.

Trying to avoid Mary Jane's grave is tricky, however. Her ancient headstone was removed years ago, evidently in an effort to save it from the clutches of vandals. In fact, the exact burial spots of all three witches are unknown.

Of the 67 tombstones that once stood in Loon Lake Cemetery, only 18 remain today. And of those 18, the inscriptions are so badly weathered that it's impossible to make out who's who. Some say this is also the work of the witches' curse—a way of upping the stakes so to speak.

While the combination of a remote location and swampy, inhospitable terrain is enough to keep most curiosity seekers away from the long-abandoned cemetery, dedicated ghost hunters have been successful in trekking to the graveyard, which is inaccessible by car. And those who have been to Loon Lake Cemetery came away with the distinct impression that the witches weren't the only spirits haunting the cemetery. The ghost hunters said they could detect plenty of other anguish as they traipsed through the grounds.

Indeed the earliest official burial in Loon Lake Cemetery was recorded in 1851, some 30 years before Mary Jane and the other witches were executed. And most of the people buried there were ordinary residents of the nearby farming communities of Jackson and Petersburg.

While there is no record anywhere of a person having died as a direct result of visiting Loon Lake Cemetery, it is possible that luck was on their side and they missed trodding upon the witches' graves. Or could it be that no one has lived to tell?

Ann Bilansky

Ann Bilansky gained notoriety in life as the first woman executed in the state of Minnesota. She hasn't lost her momentum in death either, as visitors to St. Paul's Calvary Cemetery can attest to.

The young and comely Ann was convicted of the murder of her elderly husband, Stanislaus Bilansky, in 1859. Ann was Stanislaus's fourth wife; the previous three divorced him on the grounds that he was a batterer.

The first governor of Minnesota, Henry Sibley, would not condemn a woman to death.

Whether or not Ann actually murdered her husband is still open to debate, but the fact is that she did purchase a quantity of arsenic a few days prior to Stanislaus's death. At her trial, Ann claimed she purchased the arsenic to take care of a rat problem. Her husband's official cause of death, meanwhile, was a stomach ailment.

Ann was convicted of murder in 1859 and sentenced to death by hanging. But Minnesota's first governor, Henry

Sibley, refused to sign her execution order, citing it improper to condemn a lady to death, even one who had committed a murder.

In 1860, Alexander Ramsey became Minnesota's second governor. Unlike his predecessor, Ramsey was not squeamish about signing Ann's execution order.

Alexander Ramsey, Minnesota's second governor, signed the execution order for Ann Bilansky.

The night before her death, Ann converted to Catholicism. The act was performed by Archbishop Grace. Because of her conversion, the Catholics could not forbid her body from being buried in Cavalry Cemetery. However, they did not want it known that the cemetery harbored the remains of a convicted murderess. So they did not mark Ann's grave with a headstone.

Apparently this decision did not sit well with Ann. Her ghost was often seen walking the cemetery grounds in her black execution robe, searching for the missing marker.

Anxious to bring peace to the restless spirit, the cemetery quietly erected a tombstone for Ann in the 1940s. Her ghost hasn't been seen since.

A Mother's Revenge

Mothers are able to move heaven and earth when the lives of their children are at stake. They are also capable of seeking revenge against those responsible for putting their offspring in harm's way. At St. John's University in St. Cloud, a mother's anguished vengeance for her only son is still felt more than 120 years after his accidental death.

On October 9, 1880, Brother Leo Martin was killed during the construction of the new abbey church at St. John's. Brother Martin was removing boards from scaffolding when a falling plank struck him on the head and knocked him 50 feet to the ground. For three hours he lingered between life and death, uneasy because his triennial vows had expired one month earlier. Then Abbot Alexis Edelbrock gave him his final profession and, it is reported, Martin died in peace.

Upon receiving the news of his death, Brother Martin's grief-stricken mother arrived at the abbey and demanded an explanation. The widow planned to berate the abbot for not seeing that the proper medical treatment was administered after the accident. But Abbot Edelbrock rudely refused to grant her audience, and the mother vowed to return.

Months rolled by and the new church was finally finished. At the dedication ceremony, the bereaved mother ran out of the congregation and confronted the abbot. The abbot had her thrown out of the building. Amid loud curses, she once again vowed to return. But as she drove her buggy back home, she lost control and the vehicle upturned in one of the lakes surrounding the campus. The mother drowned.

Afterwards, the wind would suddenly blast open the door of the church, and wet footprints would appear down the center aisle and stop at the altar. Despite repeated exorcisms, the same eerie event repeated itself until 1961, when the church was desanctified and a new abbey was built to replace it. As the new building was dedicated, persons knowledgeable about the curse awaited further recurrences.

During the ceremony nothing happened, but later in the day a huge crack appeared down the center aisle in the new building, a phenomenon attributed to Brother Martin's vengeful mother.

Ghosts of a Government Center

The Hennepin County Government Center is said to be haunted by the spirits of four people who died there between 1976 and 1982 after jumping from the interior bridges of the twin-tower building.

Cleaning staff and maintenance workers in particular have reported unusual events in the government center at night, from disembodied voices heard in empty rooms to wispy, ghostlike figures seen in the hallways.

But some of the hauntings seem to predate the building, which was erected in 1974. According to an article written by John Brewer of the *Southwest Journal* in Minneapolis, one employee saw two people dressed in Victorian-era clothing sit at a table and then disappear. That same employee reported hearing a sneeze in an empty elevator.

A cleaning person says he has heard a man's voice call his name from the darkened corners of empty rooms. And in one courtroom, he reportedly saw what looked like a man's shadow looming behind a judge's bench. He turned on the lights in time to see the figure slowly fade out, the state flag billowing in its ghostly wake.

A Vignette of Fright

Very rarely in the making of this book did I encounter people who had put their ghostly experiences to pen and paper. And those who did write of their encounters seldom did so in a manner that truly captured the terror of the experience. But this story by Camden freelance writer Ione Green Woodford is about as good as it gets.

Here is her story as it appeared in the November 2001 issue of the *Camden Community News*. It is reprinted with the newspaper's permission.

I had a gift shop in Camden. It was located in an aging, pie-shaped edifice adjacent to a movie theater. Other stores and offices occupied equally old buildings south to the end of the block. I thought of my establishment as a caboose at the rear of this train of businesses chugging along to an unknown destination.

Many nights after closing time I would lock the front door (the back door was always bolted) and go to the basement to sort out new merchandise and price it. Here a huge, antiquated furnace commanded a large area and the walls were barren, moldering cinder blocks. Nevertheless, it was a useful storage and workspace.

[The basement] had no windows and so, day or night, I relied on two bare lightbulbs hanging from the ceiling for illumination. A third one near the stairway was defunct. I tried fresh bulbs in the socket, to no avail, and so I finally called in an electrician to repair it. His conclusion was that, since the fixture was attached to the ceiling and badly corroded, it would need extensive rewiring to make it functional. I decided that the lighting I already had would be sufficient.

This basement was not a warm, pleasant place to work. I felt some uneasiness there and, sometimes, I would hear muffled footsteps. However, with the theater next door, I decided that these sounds originated there with their patrons moving about.

Then one night, while unwrapping a gift shipment, I heard them again—footsteps—this time immediately above me, the floor squeaking with every step. For a moment I was perplexed, but this quickly gave way to a paralyzing fear. Someone must have broken into the store by the front door or the windows.

In a cold sweat I broke out of my inertia and bolted up the stairs, knowing that it would be better to face whoever was up there than to be trapped in the basement. I peered into the back room office. No one there. I carefully scanned the main room of the store. No one. I checked the front door. Still locked, no windows broken. The lavatory! I quietly opened the door, snapped on the light. Empty. And no sound of footsteps anywhere!

I breathed a sigh of relief and resumed my work in the basement, trying to rationalize the origin of this frightening episode. Then it happened again—the measured footsteps and squeaking floor—right above me! My one thought was that I must have missed some shadowy part of the store on my first inspection.

Once again with sheer dread I rushed up the stairs, checked every possible cranny. No one.

Returning to the basement, I began wondering about the soundness of my mind. I was constantly tired and the extensive hours of work could be taking their toll. Could all this be the result of an over-wrought brain?

Just then the walking and squeaking pattern started again. I hesitated this time, listening, but not for long. Once more I ran up the stairs, almost in anger, repeated the search and, thankfully, found no one.

Enough of this. Time to go home. First, I needed to turn off the lights in the basement. Halfway down the steps I stopped. Something was different. The whole area seemed brighter than it ever had been. I stared in disbelief. It couldn't be, but there it was, the bulb in the defunct fixture shining brightly, radiantly!

I ran from that place. With hands shaking uncontrollably, I managed to lock the front door behind me and step into the welcoming darkness of the parking lot next to the store. I located my car and, somehow, was able to drive home.

The next morning, reluctantly, I went to the basement to turn off the lights. The two bare bulbs hanging from the ceiling were still burning brightly. The "defunct" fixture was dark. It never gave out a light again.

And I? I never, ever again worked at night down in that baffling, terror-filled netherworld!

The Hanging of John Moshik

The ghost of John Moshik, leader of St. Paul's notorious Rice Street Gang, is said to have haunted Minneapolis City Hall since March 18, 1898, the day he was hanged for murdering a man he'd robbed of a paltry $14.

And in November 2001 the local historical society asked John Savage and his Minnesota Paranormal Investigative Group to do a walk-through of Minneapolis City Hall to either confirm or debunk the ghost's existence.

"I think in the back of their minds they were hoping we wouldn't find anything," says Savage. "[For] the moment we told them what we had, they put a kibosh on everything."

Footage taken by the local television station during the walk-through never made it to air, a media session was cancelled and any future discussion regarding what went on that day was quashed by the historical society board once it was made aware of Savage's findings.

While Savage suspects the awful secret he uncovered about John Moshik's death partially explains the society's reaction, he believes the bottom line is that the government just isn't interested in endorsing the existence of ghosts.

"I can see their point that they are a government agency and, as such, if they were to start saying, 'Yes, this place is haunted,' some members of the public might not take kindly to that," he says. "But it also disappointed me because it showed me how narrow-minded these people are."

Moshik was the last man to be hanged in Hennepin County and the only man ever hanged in city hall. Savage began looking for him on the building's sixth floor in what is essentially now an attic. In 1898, that space housed the original jail cells and was situated directly over the spot on the fifth floor where 25-year-old Moshik was hanged in a temporary gallows set up just east of the Fifth Street Tower.

Savage says it was a challenge to find the ghost of Moshik while dragging around a camera crew and a member of the historical society, but he did accomplish his goal after just a few minutes. And at once his entire crew was overwhelmed by a sense of distrust. "There was a big group of us and he [the ghost] thought we were coming to hang him again," Savage says.

The investigator was able to convince the ghost that the group was not a lynch mob and calm it down enough to start communicating with it. "As we were talking I was trying to get some validation that this was John Moshik," Savage says, noting that he relayed the information from the ghost to the historical society member, who was there to confirm any details they might get from the ghost.

But then a funny thing happened. Savage became quite ill moments after establishing the identity of the ghost as John Moshik. And others in the group began picking up a very deep sickening feeling at the same time.

Savage began experiencing the last wretched moments of the convicted murderer's life—an experience that has left him shaken to this day. "There's nothing like reliving a hanging," he says. "I had the sensation of something around my neck and it was choking me to the point of a gagging reflex."

Savage got the impression that Moshik was actually hanged twice. He felt the noose coming loose and slipping under his jaw. "After they kicked the chair away the rope was loose and it slipped," he says. "So instead of it being around his neck and choking his wind pipe, the rope slipped up under his chin and gagged him.

"I got a sense of my mouth being blocked. (The historical society person confirmed that at the time criminals' mouths were taped shut so they wouldn't scream.) I also sensed that when he was gagging he was upchucking at the same time and because his mouth was blocked he was choking on his own vomit. When they found this out, they [rehanged] him, so he suffered twice."

Savage says the historical society member confirmed that some of the details he provided were not public knowledge. This part of the Savage's encounter is especially interesting considering the history of the building. The courtroom where Moshik was sentenced, though long ago remodeled, has claimed its share of victims.

Judge William Gunn collapsed in the doorway and never set foot in the room again. His predecessor, Judge Michael Dillon, fell violently ill while using the courtroom and later died. And prior to that, a Hennepin County attorney passed away in the chamber after suffering a heart attack while delivering his closing argument.

More recently, a city hall employee is said to have found a framed picture lying on the floor, its glass shattered and covered in blood. When the employee returned with the equipment needed to clean up the mess, however, the picture was back on the wall and in perfect condition. The photo was that of the judge who ordered Moshik's hanging.

It was easy for Savage to understand Moshik's animosity for judges once he communicated with the criminal. "I sensed that he felt his punishment didn't [fit] the crime," Savage says. "He felt he was used as a political ploy, that someone wanted to make an example of him. He was having a hard time understanding why he was judged so harshly when that kind of thing went on all the time."

A paranormal investigator had a terrifying experience at Minneapolis City Hall, thanks to the ghost of a man who was hanged there.

Savage and his crew were not able to convince the highly suspicious Moshik to move on into the light. And because of his experience in city hall, Savage is not sure he even wants to go back and try, which would leave Moshik free to continue haunting the historic building.

That's bad news for maintenance workers, some of whom refuse to go into parts of the structure after dark.

Drowning Monk

The picturesque Stella Maris Chapel on the shore of Sagatagan Lake at St. John's University in St. Cloud is a peaceful place where many come to seek solace or refuge from a busy life. That serenity is occasionally shattered, however, by the terrible sounds of thrashing water and desperate cries for help.

Yet no matter how many times in the past 111 years people have raced to the lakeshore in search of a drowning man, no one has ever been found struggling in the mirror-calm waters of the Sagatagan. No one living anyway.

The Stella Maris Chapel is haunted by the spirit of an unfortunate monk who drowned in the lake in 1890, pulled under the water by the weight of his own cassock. Brother Anselm Bartolome and a student, Felix Nelles, were ferrying sod to the chapel when the boat they were in suddenly capsized about 100 feet from the shore. Both men were good swimmers, but Brother Bartolome became tangled in his robe, panicked and pulled Nelles under the water.

Nelles struggled with Brother Bartolome and finally managed to free himself and make his way to the shore. Brother Bartolome drowned. His body was not recovered until 10 PM the next day.

Since then many people have reported hearing the splashing sound of a drowning person as they canoe on the water or walk near the area. When they investigate the noise, however, everything becomes quiet.

Others have claimed to see a black-robed figure walking down a hall and into one of the monastic cells, leaving behind a trail of wet footprints. One monk even followed the figure into the room. He was surprised to find nothing but empty space.

The Stella Maris Chapel, originally built in 1872 by monks and St. John's University students, burned to the ground in 1903 after being struck by lightning. The current chapel was built in 1916 and refurbished in 1944 and 1988.

An interesting aside to this story has to do with the ringing of a church bell. It is said that on a Holy Saturday evening many years ago, a monk stepped into the monastic gardens for a breath of fresh air. As he enjoyed the cool breeze blowing in from the lake he thought he heard a bell ringing. This was unusual because all bells were traditionally silenced from Holy Thursday through Easter Eve.

Eventually the monk realized the sound was not coming from the church but from the shore of the lake. More members of the community gathered to listen, and collectively it was decided that the ringing was coming from the chapel and that it was probably caused by children playing.

This satisfied everyone present until one of the clerics commented that there was no bell at the chapel. Suddenly the ringing stopped.

Edelbrock Haunting

Raging nationalism, political alliances and plenty of liquor were said to be at the heart of a deadly dispute that haunts the St. Cloud Hotel to this day.

On July 4, 1856, St. Cloud Hotel owner Anton Edelbrock held an Independence Day dance at the resort and invited town residents to join the celebration. Unfortunately, during the event an argument erupted over who should control the dance, the Germans or the American-born guests from nearby Sauk Rapids.

Caught up in the dispute were locals Henry Becker and Clemens "the sailor" Mulman. The pair joined the massive brawl that ensued, and Mulman eventually beat Becker senseless, pounding his head into a bloody pulp. Becker's injuries were so severe that he died several days later, reportedly after having never regained consciousness.

As St. Cloud did not yet have its own jail, Mulman was sent to St. Anthony Falls in St. Paul for confinement. He escaped, however, and was never recaptured. Some say that 150 years later Becker is still scouring the streets of St. Cloud looking for Mulman, who quite literally got away with murder.

Ghost Bear

In 1867, long before live animal mascots became politically incorrect, students at St. John's University in St. Cloud adopted a black bear named Murro as their symbolic pet. Murro had the run of the institution. He was fed from the kitchen and slept in a bed. On June 2, however, all that changed.

On that fateful summer day, student Sylvester Sheire of St .Paul teased the bear one too many times. Murro turned on Sheire and chased him into Lake Sagatagan. Sheire clambered into a boat and began whacking the animal with an oar. Murro climbed into the boat and mauled Sheire, killing him with a lethal bite to the throat. Murro was brought back to shore, where he was tied to a tree and shot.

Traumatic incidents have a way of shaping lives, even from beyond the grave. Students walking along the shoreline of Lake Sagatagan at St. John's University are sometimes startled by the sound of tree branches breaking. When they turn, they find themselves face-to-face with a terrified figure who has blood streaming from his face and neck.

Suddenly a wild thrashing is heard from the depths of the woods, as if a huge angry animal is approaching through the thicket. The panicked figure looks in the direction of the noise and then turns and runs towards the lake. The commotion in the bush also changes direction and continues in its pursuit of the bleeding figure.

Then all is quiet. When the witnesses run to the lake to investigate, they find nothing but the gentle lapping of waves on the shore.

Phantom Photo

The Landmark Center in St. Paul seemed like the perfect setting for Kimberly and Joseph Arrigoni's wedding. The grand interior of the magnificent 100-year-old structure more than made up for the dreary March weather outside, and the sweeping staircase provided the perfect backdrop for the bride and groom's postnuptial photos.

In one of these photos the smiling faces of the maid of honor, an usher, a ring bearer and the best woman flanked the happy couple from positions up on the second-floor balcony. At least those were the faces photographer Steve Tompkins saw when he snapped the picture—a picture that would later turn the Arrigonis' lives upside down.

"Nothing weird or unusual happened that day during the wedding or the reception, which was at the Landmark also," recalls Joseph. "It seemed like a pretty normal day—until the picture was found."

The extraordinary image captured in the photograph was initially overlooked by the Arrigonis, caught up as they were in the post-wedding jumble of compiling reprint orders for family and friends. It was also overlooked by Tompkins, who was more concerned with the photographic composition of the living than the dead. Indeed it wasn't until July, when the Arrigonis took their wedding album to a family reunion, that the significance of the photograph became clear.

Kimberly brought the album to show to a clutch of great-aunts and great-uncles, and to her niece, Jaime Ness. Jaime, 11, was flipping through the album when she noticed something strange in the photograph of Kimberly and Joseph with the wedding party on the balcony. For there, peering over the shoulder of five-year-old ring bearer Austin Letourneau, was the gray image of a man with a waxed mustache in a fine suit with a white tab collar. He was a stranger and he was dressed very much in early 20th-century garb.

Jaime looked at Kimberly and asked her if she knew there was a ghost in the photograph. "Immediately she said it was a ghost in the picture," says Kimberly. "We thought it was a shadow at first, but when we got home we looked at the proof—because the photo she saw was a copy—and sure enough, there he was."

Curious to identify this strange uninvited guest, Joseph scanned and enlarged the proof at work the next day. What he saw sent a chill down his spine. "I got goose bumps, a genuine adrenaline rush, and said, 'Wow, what is this?' " he recalls.

Joseph was able to make out quite clearly the transparent figure of a gentleman in his 30s or 40s. "You can make out his hair, eyes, ears and a collar," he says. "And on his right side, and on the right side of Austin and a little below him, you can see cathedral-style windows and you can almost see the cut of the glass."

Kimberly says knowing that a ghost attended their wedding gave her the "willies" because she didn't know why it was there. "The fact that it was above my nephew's head creeped me out," she says. "I didn't want it to be a premonition of anything bad in the future for him. But Joseph helped me turn that around and see the positive side of it."

Joseph speculated that maybe the ghost was Austin's guardian angel or perhaps it was someone they knew. Joseph thought it might be his grandfather or another dearly departed family member who simply wanted to be at their wedding.

The Arrigonis' search took them back to Tompkins at his photography studio in Chaska. Without divulging their incredible discovery, Kimberly asked Tompkins if he would make a partial print from the negative and then enlarge the image. But the odd request piqued Tompkins's curiosity and he asked the couple what the fuss was all about.

The Arrigonis explained rather hesitantly about the ghostly figure in the photograph. They said that they wanted it enlarged so they could take a better look at it. Unaware of the figure until that moment, Tompkins took a closer look at the photo in the area the Arrigonis were pointing to. He was taken aback by what he saw. The figure was leaning over the edge and appeared to be looking straight at him while everyone else was looking at the bride and groom.

"There's an image of a man with a receding hairline, dark hair and possibly sideburns," Tompkins says. "You can make out his eyes, nose, mouth, neck and part of his shoulder. The figure is 50 percent transparent but is so clear you could almost recognize him in person if you saw him in a lineup."

The Arrigonis asked Tompkins if the image could be explained some other way. Perhaps there was a defect on the film or a shadow was cast from someone in the wedding party. Tompkins explained that an extra image on the film could be caused by a double exposure, but that that was not the situation here. He also discounted the idea of it being a shadow or even a blur, as the wedding party was posing rather than moving when the photo was taken.

Tompkins used a magnifier to examine the photograph. However, the ghostly image diffused under magnification into a bluish-gray discoloration. Closer examination of the actual negative revealed a faint deformity of some kind on the film in the exact area where the ghost was. The anomaly didn't appear on any other negatives, including a photograph taken at the staircase just 15 seconds prior to the one that captured the ghost.

The ghost of the Landmark Center apparently joined the wedding photo session for a newly married couple.

Curiously, it was because of Austin that Tompkins had had to take the second photo. For the first one, the young ring bearer had been looking not at the bride and groom, as he was supposed to, but at the bridesmaid.

Tompkins, who describes himself as a cut-and-dried, no-nonsense kind of guy, says the photograph has convinced him that ghosts exist. "I've been in this business since 1984 and I've never seen anything like it," he says. "I don't know who this is, but I know it's definitely somebody and they are there. This image is something that even the most logical person can't dispute."

Excited about the authenticity of the photo, Joseph called the wedding coordinator at the Landmark Center and told her about the ghost in the photo. She asked him to bring the photo in so she could take a look. When he arrived, 40 employees—almost the entire Landmark staff—were waiting for him. It seems the Arrigonis' photographer had captured the ghost of the Landmark Center on film.

"They were waiting for me to get in there with this picture because of all the weird stuff that had been going on there," Joseph says. "The guys in the boiler room were saying that carts had been pushed into them. A girl in the archive room told me how every morning she walks up to the elevator and the doors automatically open and the floor number that she needs…is already lit up when she steps inside."

Joseph discovered that the section of the Landmark Center where the ghost was captured on film was a judge's office when the building served in its original function as a federal courthouse. The judge's lounge would have extended to where the balcony stands today. And, oh yes, the office had cathedral windows.

Pam Sicard has been the events coordinator for Minnesota Landmarks—the company that manages the

Landmark Center—for the better part of 17 years. While she has never seen the Landmark ghost, Sicard says she has sensed a physical presence over the years, a presence she describes as heavy, negative, agitated, irritable and mean-spirited.

She is relieved that Tompkins captured on film the ghost she and her co-workers have dealt with for so long. Although Sicard disputes the Arrigonis' claim that they can see cathedral windows in the photograph (she believes the windows are actually reflections of cathedral windows on the other side of the building that somehow bounced off the elaborate long-hanging brass sconces on the ceiling), she has no doubts about the authenticity of the figure.

"In terms of who or what we really have here, [from the photograph] we know he's a 40- to 50-year-old gentleman with a receding hairline and a mustache," she says. "And from my experiences I can tell you that he's mean. He has slammed doors behind me and pushed bar carts into me. [One] time I was standing behind one of the heavy oak planters we have here during setup and the planter was pushed into me so hard it cut my foot."

The spirit is fond of the bar area, Sicard says, especially during parties. In her years overseeing the banquet and bar service at weddings, dances and other public or corporate functions, the spirit has pushed shot glasses off the bar, broken entire trays of champagne glasses and knocked over bottles of liquor—usually gin.

He occasionally shows himself during these functions, especially to women in the second-floor washroom. As recently as July 2001, two women came out of that washroom crying and demanding that security be called because they had seen a ghost. "Granted they had had a few drinks," says

Sicard. "But they were really frightened. They said there was a man in the bathroom and that when they talked to him he disappeared right in front of their eyes."

Another incident involved a female employee who was riding in the building's glass-topped elevator reserved for people with disabilities. The worker came running out of the elevator as white as a sheet, swearing that someone had put an arm around her and breathed down her neck while she rode to the main floor. "She came flying out of that elevator and she was shaking all over, clearly frightened," Sicard says. "The spirit seems to have a fondness for pretty women and it likes the bar area—places where there are liquor, ladies and elevators."

Indeed the elevators appear to be the most consistent—and perhaps most important—part of the haunting. There are three elevators in the building. Sicard says the main public elevator is always opening as people walk by, even when no one has pushed the button to open it. And the freight elevator, for employee use only, travels to the sixth floor no matter what button is pushed.

The weird thing is that the sixth floor is a dark, rarely used locked storage space that can't be accessed from the freight elevator, Sicard says. That means someone needs to be on the sixth floor to push the button to call the freight elevator up there. "You push B to go down but it brings you up to the sixth floor. It's an eerie feeling because nobody is up there to push it."

The third elevator, the glass-topped elevator, has had the most visible hauntings. In 1985 or 1986, well-known St. Paul history buff and onetime Landmark tour guide Woodrow Keljik wrote in an internal newsletter about two tourists who saw what they described as a ghost riding it. The tourists were on the third floor looking down at the activity below when they saw through the elevator's glass ceiling a man wearing a bellhop's uniform. When the elevator reached their floor, however, it was empty. The bellhop was gone.

"I don't remember the names of the men or where they were from," Keljik told the *Pioneer Press*. "But they were serious and they were courteous. They were not making anything up."

The bellhop sighting and the spirit's apparent fondness for elevators could be important in identifying the ghost of the Landmark Center. Sicard began calling the spirit Jack after coming across some gangster-era literature chronicling the activities of legendary Prohibition-era gangster John "Jack" Peifer, who began his career as a hotel bellhop and, among other things, a carnival worker.

Peifer later became an important banker and hospitality merchant, running the Hollyhock Speakeasy on River Road, a cheeky place where gangsters and St. Paul's elite mingled over drinks of bathtub gin. Indeed it was Peifer who targeted brewery heir William Hamm to be kidnapped by the notorious Barker-Karpis gang in 1933, a role that would later earn him a date at the federal courthouse, the present-day Landmark Center.

The third floor of the courthouse was the scene of many sensational gangster trials during the 1930s, and Peifer's was no exception. He was tried and convicted in 1936 for his role as the point man in the famous kidnapping and sentenced to 30 years of hard labor at Leavenworth Prison.

But Peifer never made it to Leavenworth. Evidently upset at the harshness of his sentence, he committed suicide upon returning to his cell at the Ramsey County jail, ingesting what was believed to have been potassium cyanide. His ghost is said to have returned to the federal courthouse to avenge his horrible sentence.

After seeing the Arrigonis' photograph, however, Sicard isn't so convinced that the ghost is that of Peifer. Peifer was a clean-shaven, bland-looking sort of guy, and he didn't look anything like the man in the picture. Still, employees at the Landmark Center have been calling the spirit Jack for so long that she doubts a name change is coming anytime soon.

"For the last 14 years or so it has been very common for janitors to say, 'Get out of here, Jack' when buckets spill and dump, or for bartenders to say, 'Leave us alone, Jack' when shot glasses break or gin bottles fall over," Sicard says.

Sicard notes that she gave Jack an ultimatum of her own one summer after five or six trays of champagne glasses were inexplicably shoved off the bar during a set up for a wedding. It was the last straw, she says.

"I was fed up, so I sat down on the stairs and said, 'Damn it, Jack, I can't take it anymore. I'm alive and working here, and you are dead and you can go get out of here, so go!' Since then I haven't had an elevator door open for me, and they used to open for me four to five times a day."

While Sicard is glad the spirit has granted her at least a temporary reprieve, she does admit it would be nice to know who he was. And she may yet get a chance to find out—the elevator doors are still opening for some employees.

For now, however, there is peace—and proof that Sicard isn't out of her mind. Even if her boss, David Lanegran, president of Minnesota Landmarks, isn't so sure. Lanegran says he doesn't believe in ghosts. He thinks the spirit is a figment of Sicard's imagination.

But as Joseph points out, more than 70 people at Lanegran's workplace have seen the photograph and not one person has doubted the authenticity of the image captured on film. "I'd pretty much say everybody but the guy who owns the Landmark Center believes in it," Joseph says.

5
Minnesota's Ghost Hunters

A well-developed sixth sense is either a blessing or a curse depending on one's outlook on life. Those bestowed with this special gift usually have it to varying degrees, some able to see spirits and others able only to sense them. Despite the discrepancies in their abilities, these gifted individuals all agree that with this insight comes an incredible responsibility.

Some feel obliged to guide spirits trapped here on earth to the other side, a practice popularly known as ghost busting. Others feel it is their duty to help a spirit resolve whatever problem is keeping it from moving on in peace. Some choose to simply confirm a spirit's existence in a given place, then help the property owner understand how to coexist with it.

Send-off Psychic

There is some disagreement within the psychical world as to the role of a psychic when dealing with a haunting. Some psychics feel it is their duty to confirm only that a spirit is present; others believe it is their responsibility to help earthbound spirits move on.

Minneapolis clairvoyant Jean Kellet belongs to the latter group. "My feeling is, if there is some way to help them and let them know there is some peace [somewhere else], then we should be doing that," she says. "We don't get this gift just for ourselves and our own gain."

Kellet, who started her career as a medium before moving on to ghost busting 20 years ago, says her experience has taught her that not all spirits know enough to go to the bright light at the moment of death. Accordingly, she believes there are plenty of spirits trapped in a dimension she calls the astral plane (a sort of buffer zone between life on earth and the great beyond) and will never find peace and contentment without the assistance of humans.

Kellet says the astral plane is so closely related to human existence that spirits in it keep their human form, albeit a lighter version. These anomalies are commonly referred to as ghosts.

Kellet believes there are a variety of life issues that leave spirits powerless to move beyond the astral plane. "It is said when you leave, that whatever state of being you are in is where you are going to stay," she explains. "If you weren't religious or aware through other means that there is a place of peace beyond this life, you will fall into a state of just existing [on the astral plane]. You will not aspire to peace or heaven and go to the light, or if you do go to the light, you will only go so far."

The astral plane can be a trap, Kellet says. Spirits can be caught in it for a very long time—perhaps indefinitely. Such was the case in a home Kellet investigated in the Linden Hills area of Minneapolis.

The case involved a couple who bought a beautiful 1880s-era mansion. The house had gained some notoriety in the mid-1980s when it underwent a complete renovation courtesy of the popular PBS television show "This Old House." But nothing could compare to what took place when the family moved in.

Almost immediately the couple's three young children refused to sleep in their own rooms, complaining that they could hear muffled screams coming from behind the walls. They were convinced someone who didn't belong there was in the house. The mother, too, felt uncomfortable in the home but didn't call Kellet until she saw the ghostly figure of an older woman hurrying down the second-floor hallway and then disappearing into thin air.

The children's rooms were on the third floor of the house. Prior to the renovation, this area was the servant's quarters and was accessible only through a steep and narrow staircase concealed in the back part of the house. The staircase had been walled-in during the renovations, sealing the section running between the second and the third floors behind the back wall of a dressing room/walk-in closet in the master bedroom on the second floor.

It was on this back wall that the couple had installed sturdy new steel rods on which to hang their clothing. The day before Kellet arrived to start her investigation, the rods had come down off the wall with all the clothes on them.

Instead of finding gaping holes in the plaster where the rods had been secured to the wall, the couple was stunned to find that the wall had been ripped out in the shape of the stairs.

When Kellet arrived, she sensed that the presence of spirits was strongest by this wall and so she began her investigation there.

Rather than seeing ghosts, Kellet detects them through physical sensations. In a typical case, she is overcome by a feeling of heaviness, a racing heart and the sensation of a presence inside her. "It's not an uplifting or inspiring feeling," she says. "We feel their emotional heaviness and sometimes experience their physical pain in cases where they died of a traumatic injury, and that's generally a clue that they are in some distress. They are not going to bother people unless they want some relief."

This is what Kellet experienced in spades when she entered the master bedroom dressing room. "I was getting more and more weird impressions and was being overwhelmed and had to leave the room," she says. "I went and sat down in the living room and all of a sudden I could feel myself about to scream. The rage was so intense that I literally felt like I was about to come out of the chair."

What Kellet had picked up on was the spirit of a child, either mentally challenged or autistic, with some physical problem, such as a heart condition. "He was out of control and in a rage and the father had sent him into the staircase for punishment and he died there," she says. "[I sensed] it was hot in there and he died from a combination of the heat, his heart condition and fright."

Kellet also sensed the presence of an older woman and a man. She was able to identify the woman as the boy's maid. The man turned out to be his father.

The boy's spirit had been trapped in the astral plane, suspended in the last awful moments of his life for more than 100 years, because he was too young to realize what had happened to him or how to move on. The father, whom Kellet later identified as an attorney, was stuck in the astral plane out of tremendous guilt over his son's death.

Kellet worked with the spirits over several days and eventually succeeded in prodding all three along to the light. "Eventually the problem went away and the wall went back up," she says.

Guilt and a lack of spiritual knowledge are not the only things that keep spirits languishing in the astral plane. Those so attached to loved ones or worldly possessions that they can't let go will also stay there indefinitely. Another haunting in Linden Hills that Kellet investigated is a perfect example of this situation.

In this case, a 1900s mansion had been turned into an apartment building. "People on the third floor kept seeing the face of an old man peering in the window. They were pretty spooked."

Kellet was able to determine that the spirit belonged to be the original homeowner, who was very attached to the building. He had lived there nearly all his life, refusing to move out even when he was gravely ill. And when he died he still did not want to leave. "We were able to prompt him on and let him know that this house wasn't all he had," she says.

Cases like this, where rooting out the cause of a haunting is a challenge, underscore why Kellet is such an advocate of personal development for psychics. "If we don't develop ourselves, we're not going to be able to give any information other than the mundane, and most people don't want to

know if they are going to get married or where their grandmother's brooch is," she says.

Indeed spirits often make themselves known when they
are upset about something, and it's the psychic's job to determine what that is. One particular case Kellet investigated near
Minnehaha Falls took place in a house where strange things
had been going on. Cupboard doors kept opening, the normally staid family dog had became high-strung and nervous
and the woman's jewelry was disappearing piece by piece.

Kellet discovered that the house was built on sacred
ground and that the spirit belonged to an American Indian.
She also found out the ghost was taking her client's jewelry to
display his immense displeasure with her presence on his
grave site.

"He somehow needed [for it] to be acknowledged that
this was the spot," Kellet says. "My client couldn't move the
house, so it was as simple as getting her to honor the spot."
The woman accomplished this by doing a ritual five days in a
row. "[Then] one day she called me up screaming, saying
she'd come home to find all her missing jewelry on her
dresser. Since then, the dog has calmed down and the cupboard doors have stayed closed."

Not all spirits are so easily appeased, however. If the spirit
involved met with a violent death, communicating with it
telepathically can be a physically and emotionally taxing
ordeal. "There have been occasions with…things happening
in places where there have been violent murders," Kellet says.
"It's a very scary thing and something I experienced in
another Linden Hills home."

In this case, the client was house-sitting. Whenever she
entered the basement she was overcome with an uneasy feeling. Kellet believed that someone had been killed in the

home's basement and that the spirit of that person was stuck there, absolutely traumatized.

In addition to the overwhelming sense of unease, the client's boyfriend, who had also been staying in the house, saw the ghost of a woman on the second floor. He was so "freaked out" he refused to stay in the house.

Kellet did some work with the spirits and convinced them to move on. Their departure made such a difference in the atmosphere of the home that when the homeowners returned they immediately sensed the change. "They asked my client what she did," Kellet says. "They had noticed the presence in their home but didn't know something could be done about it and so had decided to live with it. Needless to say they were grateful."

Spirits can have a powerful influence, both spiritually and physically, on the people whose homes they are haunting. Kellet encountered one example of this in an older home in Minnetonka, where the spirit of a deranged man was tearing an otherwise normal family apart. As Kellet explained, "The couple was having a lot of difficulties in their relationship and the home was causing the problems."

Kellet recalls entering the home and being immediately drawn to an area of the house with a "different, uncomfort-able cold feel to it…Up above this spot was the sitting room and below it was their son's bedroom. Their son was having challenges. At times he was just not himself because he was really affected. The whole area of the house on that side was showing the effects of the spirit."

Kellet was able to determine that the spirit was a male and was very disturbed. The emotions she experienced ranged from restlessness to agitation, from anger to disappointment to fear. There was also a lot of confusion and distress.

"He must have been psychologically unstable and a very unhappy person because of the instability," Kellet says. "The person had lived there and just could not find any peace. I think he really wanted to connect with somebody in the house and, unfortunately, he was not a good spirit to connect with."

Kellet says this type of situation is exactly what psychics were meant to remedy. Simply acknowledging that the spirit existed would have doomed it to an eternity of unrest and would have left the family in a situation of irreparable harm. And those results were not acceptable to Kellet.

Kellet also urges psychics to hone their craft so they are accurate in their readings. She feels so strongly about this because of two clients who came to her after receiving deeply disturbing readings from another psychic. Although the clients were not related, their readings were identical. The psychic claimed they had been sexually abused by their fathers and had repressed the memories.

Kellet investigated the psychic on behalf of the distraught women and discovered that it was the psychic who had been sexually abused, and that she was exporting her own experiences onto her clients. "It made me wonder how many other clients this woman had given this information to," Kellet says.

She adds, "You have a big responsibility when you have this gift. You have to work on yourself and your own psychic development so your emotions don't fog the outcome. A lot of psychics do this. We are not always accurate in our readings but it frightens me to think of what was going on with that woman for so long. This is what pushed me to investigate more."

Ghost Buster with a Gift

If there's one thing John Savage of the Minnesota Paranormal Investigative Group has learned over the years, it's that ghosts don't like being ignored.

"Ghosts are trying to get your attention," he says. "Either there's something that they're trying to tell you, or they just want you to acknowledge that they're there. The worst thing you can do is ignore [a ghost], especially if the spirit is very active. You have to consider it as you would a two-year-old child, and we all know what happens when you ignore a two-year-old."

Since forming in St. Paul in 1997, Savage's group has taken on some of the state's most challenging hauntings. The team got its start in old cemeteries doing spirit photography and so on, and progressed to investigating buildings and old homes and locations, such as American Indian burial grounds.

The crew blends Savage's psychic abilities with scientific data gathered from electromagnetic field meters, night-vision cameras and thermal guns for detecting, measuring and tracking cold spots. It boasts an enviable record as Minnesota's premier ghost-buster team, and is in heavy demand.

Savage provides his service free of charge. He seeks only to help people cope with sharing their house with a ghost. It's a subject close to his heart. He's been able to encounter ghosts from a very young age, a gift that has not always been appreciated by his deeply religious parents.

"I'm an army brat and have lived all over the world and have seen many ghosts, but my parents always told [me] that ghosts were evil," he says. "I [ghost bust] to develop my psychic abilities but also to help people cope with living in a house that is haunted. So I do this as a gift."

Some of Savage's clients simply seek confirmation that their house is haunted; others request that he and his group expel the spirits from the residence. But that isn't always possible.

"If a spirit doesn't want to go, we can't force it to, because there is such a thing as free will," Savage says. "If the ghost wants to stay, we will help the client establish boundaries inside the home, such as where it is allowed to stay, and [we'll teach] techniques [to] families to help the children cope with having a ghost in the house."

Savage's numerous experiences have led him to the conclusion that most hauntings are the handiwork of deceased relatives keeping an eye on loved ones, sort of like guardian angels. But there are several other reasons that ghosts linger in this life. In the course of his ghostly investigations, Savage has come across matters of religious beliefs, of sudden and tragic deaths leaving a spirit confused and unaware that it is dead, of unfinished business, of concerns over how a family member will cope with the death, and of worries over family heirlooms.

Indeed, the whereabouts of a treasured heirloom was at the bottom of a haunting Savage investigated in an early 20th-century residence along the bluffs on the east side of St. Paul. The homeowner complained of having the constant sensation of someone watching her. Savage identified the spirit as that of the homeowner's Italian grandmother. He drew this conclusion after visiting the house and being struck with a vision of St. Peter's Square.

"I got an image of smoke, a rosary and a piece of paper," Savage says. "The homeowner went to her mother and talked it over with her. It turns out the grandmother had been to St. Peter's [Square] to see the new pope, and had had her rosary blessed by the pope and also received a house blessing, which is on a piece of paper with the Vatican's coat of arms on it."

The images Savage saw, which he describes as being similar in appearance to those on an incredibly slow and choppy 8-millimeter film, helped him to determine that the spirit belonged to the grandmother and that she wanted to know where the items were.

Savage was also called in to investigate the strange goings-on in a 114-year-old mansion in St. Paul's Highland Park. This homeowner complained that lights would turn on and off by themselves, that the doorbell would ring when no one was there and that someone was playing with her dog—although it was quite clear there was no human presence around.

Savage's investigation turned up three ghosts in the house. The first he identified as "Billy," the deceased brother of the homeowner. "Billy died in a car accident right after returning home from the Vietnam War," he says. "He was there in a caretaker role to look after his sister."

Another ghost haunting the grand staircase in the house was identified as the original homeowner who, along with his entire family, had been killed about three blocks from the house. And a ghost in a closet upstairs on the second floor remained unidentified.

Savage managed to capture the third ghost on video and audiotape. "You can see the white shirts hanging in the closet get darker and darker until the camera goes out of focus," he says. "All of a sudden you hear [from the closet], 'What?' "

Savage believes experiences like this one give him a better understanding of "what's going to happen to us when we die."

He says, "Everyone is afraid of dying, and this gives me hope that my life, or our lives in general, have a purpose here, and it gives me hope that I'm doing something right. What I'm hoping to get out of all of this is a better understanding of the unknown."

It's easy to understand Savage's quest for the truth. One of his earliest ghostly encounters occurred when he was a child living with his family in Germany. He was on an overnight outdoor campout in an old castle ruin with his Boy Scouts troop when he awoke suddenly.

"I looked across the campfire," he says, "and there were a bunch of guys…deep in conversation, wearing what I can only describe as clothing from the Middle Ages. I nudged my friends awake for them to take a look. But by the time they woke up the ghosts were gone."

Another incident in Germany occurred when he was on a tour of the Liechtenstein Castle with his family. Savage saw what he assumed was an oddly dressed male servant walk past the tour group and down the hallway. No one else in the group could see the figure when Savage pointed out its strange attire.

Savage was never scared of the ghosts he saw as a child. In fact, later on he sought training to develop his psychic abilities and open up the channels of communication with the spirit world.

Since then he's gone on to investigate a 3000-year-old American Indian burial ground located high above the Mississippi River on the east bluffs of St. Paul. The remains of members of the unknown band were buried in several large mounds on the site in the belief that the height of the cliffs would make it easier for the souls of the dearly departed to reach the heavens.

Strange things began to happen when the city began building homes near the area. Some residents reported hearing the slow, measured sound of beating drums in the middle of the night, some saw strange blue lights moving around the mounds and in a park directly across the street, and some witnessed ghostly figures of buckskin-clad men wandering through the area.

Savage believes this site is active because the sacred American Indian burial mounds were desecrated to make way for construction. During his investigation, he was able to capture on film the image of what he says appears to be a horse and a rider wearing a feather headdress.

Today the area is a county park. And a fence protects the burial mounds from further disturbance.

Savage's group has also investigated the Brewery Hill "spook light" in Le Sueur. According to local legend, a hermit once lived in the caves along the train tracks. One evening, the hermit accidentally stepped out on to the tracks—possibly in a drunken stupor—and was hit and killed by a train. Ever since, people have reported seeing a strange ball of light bounce along the tracks. And they've claimed to see the ghostly image of a man holding a lantern standing near the tracks trying to slow the train down.

While Savage didn't see either image during his investigation, one of his teammates did take a photograph that captured an orb floating right above Savage's head.

Savage has also worked on a house in Minneapolis that he describes as "very, very haunted." He says the homeowner's emotional state has left him vulnerable to ghosts. One spirit, later identified as the homeowner's great-grandfather, had committed some dastardly acts as a young man. Savage says that spirit is now trying to make amends.

Perhaps the most unusual haunting Savage has ever investigated was one that took place in a trailer park in Mankato. In this case, an aggressive male entity didn't like the husband of the home and tried his best to run him out of the trailer. It did like the wife, however, and it wanted to connect with her.

The entity proved too much for Savage, so he called in a more seasoned ghost buster. Even then the spirit refused to move on. After five intense hours in the trailer, they were left with little choice but to banish it from the site.

In Isanti, Savage investigated a frightening haunting in a residential home that got its start more than a century earlier as the local schoolhouse. Built in 1889, the Pershing School functioned until the late 1960s, when the structure was converted into apartments. Those apartments quickly became run-down, however, and eventually the building fell vacant and became a target of vandals. The basement was flooded, the walls were covered in graffiti and the windows were broken.

In 1997, the schoolhouse/apartment building was sold, and the new owner began to restore the structure and convert it into a single family home. During the renovations, the family had several encounters with spirits. They heard footsteps walking across the main floor (where the living room, kitchen, main bath and four bedrooms were located) and tapping sounds from one of the bedrooms. The family also heard the sound of someone running up and down the stairs.

In addition to the noises, lights in the house would shut on and off at random, and one room couldn't be heated no matter what was tried. "The room was always 10–15 degrees colder than the rest of the house, even in…summer," says Savage.

The family had three daughters. The girls would wake up in the middle of the night to the sound of their bedroom doors opening. One got up to close the door, only to find it open again by the time she returned to her bed. She got up to close it again, and this time she felt a force on the other side of the door pushing against her, and the doorknob turning in her hand. Terrified, she ran back into bed. When she looked back at the door, the doorknob was shaking.

On another evening, during a sleepover party, the girls saw a young girl peeking around the corner of the bathroom with her hand over her mouth as if she was giggling. They watched her run from the bathroom down the hallway to the living room, where she disappeared.

A few days later, one of the girls heard a woman and a small girl—whom she described as a "mommy and daughter"—yelling in the kitchen area.

And the children weren't the only ones who had strange encounters. One evening after the kids had gone to bed their mother heard what sounded like someone throwing wood into the furnace. When she went down into the basement to investigate, the noise stopped. She also saw the outline of an entity reflected in the glass from a display case. It appeared to be a female form but with a very dark mass to it.

Savage and his crew were able to make contact with several spirits during their investigation of this house. "One was of a teenage girl. She did not want to speak to us while we were there. We think that she was the one who was making the children scared," says Savage.

"Another entity was a woman in the basement. She was there to watch over the family and the spirit of the teenage girl. A man in the well room (located in the basement) was there because of a fight near the well. Either he was hurt or saw someone get hurt in or near the well. We also picked up several other entities outside of the schoolhouse, but were unable to gain any information on who they were."

Savage's team was able to capture on film the ghost of a woman and child in the basement. Was the child the ghost the young girl had heard arguing in the kitchen that day? The answer is anyone's guess.

Savage found several ghosts throughout the house and on the grounds, an oddity that has led him to conclude that the entities were former students. "It makes sense that they'd want to return here in death," he says, "when you think that they probably had a lot of good experiences here in life."

Deciphering Ghostly Clues

In the 1984 hit movie *Ghostbusters*, Dan Aykroyd relied on laser guns to remove unwanted spirits from homes. But real-life ghost buster and psychic Carol Lowell says little more than intuition is needed to get the job done.

"Everyone has psychic abilities," Lowell says. "Sometimes we just need someone to teach us how to recognize them."

Lowell has been ghost busting since 1991. But she's always believed in life after death. "[As a child] I even had a pretend ghost friend named George," she says. "Later I discovered that he was real; not a ghost, but one of my spirit guides."

Today Lowell's work involves helping lingering ghosts cross over to the other side. To do this, she must determine why they have not left earth in the first place. There are lots of reasons ghosts do not go into the light right after death, Lowell says. Some have family members they need to say good-bye to; others want to comfort a person having a difficult time dealing with their demise.

But lingering ghosts are not the only specters Lowell contends with. The popular ghost buster also deals with spirits who've crossed to the other side but still occasionally visit earth. These ghosts manifest themselves in a more solid spirit form, Lowell says. And they usually stay in one place—in a room, house or piece of furniture—in the same manner they were in when they passed away.

For example, one ghost-busting job Lowell took on involved the spirit of an elderly woman who had suffered from slight memory loss. That ghost was very confused. "She knew that she was dead but thought that she needed to take care of the girl that had moved into her home," Lowell says. "I had to explain to her that it was the girl who had called me and asked me to come and talk to her, and that the girl wanted her to go into the light."

These ghostly visitors are not out to cause problems, Lowell believes, but are simply attempting to communicate with living people. And the only way they can is by making loud stomping noises or moving objects around.

Ghosts become very frustrated when people can't hear them or don't understand their form of communication, Lowell adds. Especially when this communication is obvious once the clues are pieced together. One such case revolved around a phone call Lowell received from a man who had so many odd things happening in his house that he was getting desperate.

During the telephone conversation, Lowell sensed the presence of a male ghost, probably that of an older man. When she suggested this to the caller, he confirmed that was the same impression he and his wife had. "They thought they knew who it was and added that on occasion they could smell smoke in the house," Lowell says. "At that point I told [the caller] not to tell me anything else because I wanted to gather the rest of the information from the ghost."

When Lowell walked through the client's house she sensed that the ghost hung around three different rooms: the master bedroom, the living room and the basement bedroom of the couple's son. "In these three rooms his energy was the strongest," she says. "When the couple would go to bed he would go down to the son's room, and when the son would be in his room the ghost would retreat to the living room."

Lowell was in the basement when she decided to scan the house psychically to try to locate the ghost. "I could see that he was sitting on the bed in the master bedroom. I was going to talk to him psychically (with my mind) but my (spirit) guides told me to go up there and talk to him directly, so I did," she says.

"I could see [clearly] what he looked like. He told me that he was the father of my client and he showed me his heart. At first I thought he was trying to tell me that he had died of a heart attack, but that was not the case. He had tears in his eyes and said that when he died it broke his heart to leave his family. He loved them so much and didn't want to go, so he never crossed over."

Ghost buster Carol Lowell uses her psychic abilities to help lingering ghosts cross over to "the other side."

172 Ghost Stories of Minnesota

Lowell says the ghost also relayed some personal information he wanted her to share with his son. Then he told her he was getting ready to go into the light and was preparing to say good-bye. "The father had been doing all sorts of things to try and get his son's attention and make him realize that he was there," Lowell says, "but the family kept discounting all the things that were happening."

To get his son to notice him the ghost would cause electrical appliances to turn on by themselves, the smell of smoke to fill the master bedroom and a very heavy old-fashioned fire pole centerpiece in the house to simply fall over. He thought he was being obvious. After all, in life he had been a firefighter.

Investigating the Intangible

Richard Hagen says the most popular names for Minnesota ghosts are George and Albert. And he ought to know.

As founder of the Ghost Hunters Society of Minnesota, a group that investigates and chronicles ghost hauntings and sightings, the retired U.S. Air Force lieutenant colonel has examined more than 30 paranormal happenings in Minnesota over the past 10 years alone.

"You run into a lot of similarities in hauntings," he says. "There are only so many things a ghost can do."

Strict confidentiality agreements prevent Hagen from discussing specific details of his cases, but he is a good source of interesting trivia about ghosts. He gathered his information during 30 years of research in the field at home and abroad, and maintains it in one of the largest private libraries on the paranormal in the U.S.

An interesting ghostly tidbit Hagen shares has to do with age. He says ghosts can appear in a form that is younger than they were when they actually died. Hagen cites an investigation involving the ghost of Minnesota's first female superintendent of schools. That spirit appeared to the psychic to be in her 40s, when actually the woman had lived well into her 90s.

"Ghosts appear to you at an age that is most recognizable to you," Hagen says. "And when you find out [how old they were] when they died, there is usually quite a discrepancy."

But the appearance of a ghost isn't the only telltale sign of a haunting, Hagen says. A variety of paranormal activities qualify, including noises, smells, displaced objects, electrical displays and full-fledged apparitions.

When a ghost is discovered, the Ghost Hunters Society does not seek to expel it from the property, Hagen says. The group endeavors to identify it and then help the haunting make sense to the homeowner. Investigations by the society team begin with an interview of the property owner, followed by the elimination of all possible explainable causes, such as squeaky floors or faulty light switches.

"Usually if a client is concerned about things that go on in their house it's not [because they are frightened]," Hagen says. "Generally it's just a matter of somebody being curious about what's going on in their home."

After the interview, Hagen and his four-member scientific team walk the entire property, using infrared thermometers, a collection of cameras and a variety of films to measure and record activity, immediately visible or otherwise. Then, based on the results of their scientific assessment, Hagen and other investigators decide whether to bring in a psychic to make contact.

Frequently clients have unwittingly had some form of connection with the ghost already. "Clients will often have come up with a name for a ghost and then a psychic will go in and make contact and sure enough that's the ghost's name," Hagen says. "So the client was actually in contact with the ghost whether they knew it or not."

Some of the oldest ghosts Hagen and the society team have dealt with in Minnesota date back to the 1850s and 1860s. Some of the oldest they've encountered abroad—at Warwick Castle in Warwickshire, England—are more than 300 years old. "There are older ghosts too, Roman ghosts," Hagen says, "but that is the oldest we have dealt with."

Hagen recently returned from England where he spent five weeks with English ghost society chapters. There he was lucky enough to witness an illuminosity, a word he uses for an apparition. "It was almost a human form," he says, adding, "when [it is] disappearing [it] folds inwards; it just rolls in on itself and is gone. It was quite interesting to see."

Hagen also worked with Eddie Berk, a man the *London Telegraph* refers to as "England's Ghost Hunter." Hagen says "As a ghost hunter, I learned more from Eddie Berk in one day than I have from 10 years on the job...He doesn't have to go into a trance or anything. He walks into an environment and if there is something there he picks up on it and starts relating to it right off and what he gets always makes sense."

Over the past decade, Hagen has been called in to investigate just about every nook and cranny of the state of Minnesota. One such examination occurred in a Victorian river-town inn, whose name and location must remain anonymous in accordance with client confidentiality rules. The inn's owner invited the Ghost Hunters Society to investigate the property in 1993, after several guests reported spooky sightings and incidents.

One witness woke from an afternoon nap in her third-floor room to find the figure of a woman in a long gown standing over her. That guest was extremely distressed when she reported what she saw to the owner.

A second spectator, visiting from England, took her experience more in stride. She finished unpacking, then went downstairs to calmly inform the owner that there was a ghost in her assigned room. She had, it turned out, a psychic ability.

A third informant and his friend returned to their room after a late dinner and dead-bolted their door, for it would not remain shut otherwise. Then they went to bed. At 2:30 AM they were awakened by the sound of the door opening. They did not see it open, but the informant turned in time to observe it closing. He jumped out of bed and opened the door, which was no longer dead-bolted. There was no one in sight in the hallway. All the other guest doors were shut and not a sound was to be heard.

The society team held three separate investigations, involving three psychics, during the spring and summer of 1993. These investigations included two vigils, or sittings, in the haunted third floor, and a "walk-through" exploration of the house.

The first vigil began dramatically when the room was suddenly infused with the aroma of lavender, which was detected by all who were present, especially one person who was allergic to scents.

Psychic Cheryl Barnett made contact with the entity, whom she identified as "Sarah." Sarah wore a long blue-gray dress with a brooch on the bodice, and her loveliness and disposition impressed Barnett. She was gentle even though she was marked by certain frustration.

Barnett carried on a conversation with Sarah and recorded it on tape. She discovered that Sarah's sister had been fatally injured in a carriage accident and that Sarah had raised her sister's children. She also discovered that Sarah believed the children were still in the house.

Very little is known of the house's previous occupants, but the existence of Sarah and the sister's injury and subsequent death in the late 1800s were verified in newspaper archives and old public health records.

The walk-through investigation of the house was carried out with two psychics, Edith Jenks and Carol Bratter, who independently detected the existence of Sarah on the third floor. They didn't identify her by name, but by appearance and persona, which they both described as "saintly."

But this time the team was also drawn to a more disturbing energy in the first-floor sitting room next to the entrance foyer. One of the psychics was instantly repelled by the room and refused to go in. Understandable, seeing as how heightened sensitivity makes a psychic especially emotionally vulnerable to imprints in a setting, both pleasant and unpleasant.

The other psychic entered and sensed the imprint of a man with a disability. She reported that the room had been his temporary bedroom until he died there in the late 19th century. From the lingering energy it appeared the man had been a somewhat embittered occupant.

Footprints in the Snow

As co-founder of the Ghost Hunters Society of Minnesota, Alger Olson, who died in 2001, witnessed his fair share of ghosts. In 2000 Alger wrote about a paranormal event in a newsletter. This peculiar paranormal event defied all attempts at an explanation.

The incident occurred in a northern Minnesota town on a star-filled night in the month of January. It centered on a shanty-like clubhouse where Olson and his friends gathered to play cards, listen to the radio and shoot the breeze.

The snow around the clubhouse had become crusty, and for a week during the evening the club members heard the footsteps of someone or something circling the building, always in the same clockwise direction. They took no notice until twilight several days later when one of the group got up, went to the door and looked out. To his surprise the crunching suddenly stopped. The night was eerily quiet.

The group grabbed a couple of flashlights and went outside to investigate. Whoever or whatever had circled the clubhouse had mysteriously disappeared—but not without leaving a mark. On the ground, in the crusty snow illuminated by the pale light of the torches, were huge footprints that made tight but concentric circles around and around the clubhouse.

"Alarm dissolved into fear," said Olson. "One of [our] favorite pastimes during the long winter nights was to tell ghost stories. Each person had some uncanny or supernatural experience or knew of someone who did. But what we were experiencing seemed a bit too close for comfort."

A couple of nights later it snowed. The clubhouse was built on the shores of a lake, and the snow covered the ice, giving it an unblemished appearance. That evening the club members again heard the mysterious crunching sounds.

"One of the group had brought a baseball bat in case we needed to confront whoever or whatever was scaring us," Olson said. "We rushed outside [but found] the night quiet. There was no sound. But there they were, the same large footprints illuminated by our flashlights and by the light of a full pale moon."

The footprints were fresh and circled the clubhouse as they had previously done. But there was one difference. This time they led from the front door out onto the frozen lake. "[Yet] there was no one on the lake but us," Olson wrote. "How could anyone disappear so quickly?"

The group followed the footprints onto the ice. Fear slowly overtook their curiosity and they were about to return to the secure confines of the clubhouse when the tracks suddenly ended. Ahead, the snow lay flat and undisturbed. It was as if whoever or whatever had made the footprints had suddenly and inexplicably been lifted up.

"Thankfully we heard no more from our nocturnal visitor," Olson concluded. But he added that on his visits to the site of the long-dismantled clubhouse, "I feel a tingling on the back of my neck and I wonder…"

6
Legends
of Mysterious
Minnesota

Legends result when a tale is repeated enough, altered slightly on each retelling, to the point where the story becomes larger than the original incident that prompted it in the first place. The line between fact and fiction becomes blurred, with the resulting fanciful tales compelling enough to send shivers down anyone's spine. These are the tales that bear repeating around the campfire, at sleepovers and especially around Halloween. With a little creative licence added from the storyteller, the following tales are destined to become even creepier.

The Legend of the Blue Light

A freak accident in the early 1900s in Stillwater has given rise to an eerie legend that lives on to this day.

A farmer living in a house below a train bridge was reportedly employed part-time as a track checker. In those days, track checkers used a blue light in a lantern to warn oncoming engineers to slow down when rail conditions warranted caution.

One night, a train passing too quickly over the bridge above the farmer's home cast off a shower of sparks that fell onto the house and set it ablaze, burning the man's wife and animals to death. The grief-stricken farmer put a curse on the area, and that curse has stood the test of time.

Since then, the farmer's ghost has haunted the track. Frequently, at about the same time of day as the tragedy occurred, an eerie blue light is seen at the spot where the farmhouse burned to the ground. Legend has it that anyone who sees that blue light will die.

In 1968 four teenagers drove to the area on a double date and experienced the curse. Though none of them died, they all experienced a fright and some very bad luck. As the two couples got out of the car for some fresh air, they discovered all their tires were flat.

After stumbling about in the bush for an hour unsuccessfully looking for help, the foursome headed back to the car in single file. The first three teens passed through a narrow part in the path unhampered, but the fourth ran into a barbed wire fence. As the others helped untangle their friend, they saw the blue light hovering above the ground.

It was the last time any of them ever went to that spot.

Witch Tree

The ancient and gnarled cedar that grows so defiantly on a craggy cliff above Hat Point on Lake Superior has been feared by explorers of the Great Lake for well over 400 years. But the Grand Portage Ojibway believe the *Manido Giizhigance*, or Little Cedar Tree Spirit, represents sacred powers and is to be respected, not feared.

Despite its twisted and misshapen appearance, caused by enduring centuries of battering north winds on Lake Superior, Little Cedar Tree Spirit is considered by the local Ojibway to be an object of great beauty and grace. It is also believed to have the power to calm waters. For the past several hundred years, the Ojibway have shown their respect to Little Cedar Tree Spirit through regular offerings of tobacco in return for safe journeys across Lake Superior.

Today, tourists coming to the cliff's edge want to see what's been trumped up by the state's tourism industry as the Witch Tree. Although there is no witch anywhere in the region's history to corroborate the legend, the locals have made a successful pitch about the tree being possessed by evil spirits.

Crowds of gawkers have vandalized the ancient cedar, some even going so far as to carve their initials in the tree, thus disrespecting what has been a sacred place to the Ojibway for the past four centuries.

Ojibway on the Grand Portage Reservation have tried to protect Little Cedar Tree Spirit by blocking access to trails and limiting hours of visitation. However, some feel the damage has been too great and that the tree is already spiritually, if not physically, dead.

New Year's Eve Ghost

A family that died in a terrible car accident in Stillwater seems doomed to spend eternity repeating the final moments of their lives—much to the horror of modern-day witnesses. This account comes from the Ghost Hunters Society of Minnesota.

During a winter holiday break from school, at about 7 PM one evening, Megan Lynott and her friend Colleen were tobogganing in a ravine in Battle Hollow near the intersection of Laurel Street and Owen Street. The girls had stopped sliding to play on a large fallen tree when they heard a terribly loud noise that sounded as if it was just a few feet above their heads.

The pair had no idea what was making the noise, but they were very scared. They fell to the ground, huddled together. Then they ran back up the hill and dragged their sleds home.

The following Monday one of the girls reported the incident to a teacher, who happened to be a longtime resident of Stillwater. Upon hearing the story, the teacher told her student about an incident that occurred during the Christmas season in the early 1900s.

A car carrying a family of four drove across a bridge that once spanned the ravine the girls had been sledding in. The bridge was icy and the car slid and plunged over its side. Everyone in the car was killed.

It seems the girls were not the first to hear this eerie reenactment. Two years after the fatal accident a man walking in the ravine on New Year's Eve heard the loud noise, too. This man also saw a ghostly image of a car going over the side of a bridge.

Milford Mine

The worst mining disaster in Minnesota history occurred on February 5, 1924, when a shaft at the Milford Mine in Crow Wing County flooded and collapsed, burying 41 men alive.

Clinton Harris died at the bottom of the 200-foot shaft that day, choosing to stay and pull the warning whistle to alert miners higher up of the approaching disaster rather than try to save himself. And his ghost has made sure that no one ever forgets it.

Harris was working as a skip operator at the manganese mine the day miners blasted an underground shaft situated near a deep pond next to the quarry. The blast caused a huge backdraft of wind to swoop through the mine, knocking down men and short-circuiting the electric lights, plunging everything into darkness and confusion.

Seconds later, a wall of water came crashing into the shaft; the blast had ruptured the bottom of the pond, causing its contents to pour into the passageway. Panicked miners scrambled in the dark to get to the surface. Some miners died instantly, killed by the sheer force of the water, while others, weak with fatigue and fear, drowned. Only 7 of the 48 miners survived.

Realizing he was about to die, Harris tied the whistle pull around his waist, ensuring that even in death he would be saving some miners' lives.

The shrill cry of Harris's warning whistle provided an eerie backdrop to the calamity going on aboveground as workers scrambled to help their mates trapped in the shaft, now a rising torrent of mud and water. The whistle was still sounding five hours later as mud spewed out of the mouth of the shaft, and it continued issuing its woeful warning until a worker disconnected the pull, silencing the alarm forever.

The rescue effort began that evening but was hampered by a series of problems. Crews began pumping water out of the mine but the pond still contained water and simply filled in what they were pumping out. The decision was made to drain the pond, a labor-intensive process that took 12 days. By this point it was clear that the focus of the search had shifted from rescuing survivors to recovering bodies.

Once the pond was drained, the crews set about pumping water out of the shaft, a task that took another three months. Then they began the arduous job of shoveling out the mud, which was done by hand so as not to smash the decaying bodies, adding another nine months to the effort. All told, it took one year for the rescue team to recover all 41 bodies from the shaft.

The disaster was still fresh on everyone's mind when the mine reopened for business, spurred by a huge increase in demand for manganese. Local miners jumped at the chance to work again, having been unemployed for some time. But they got more than they bargained for when they entered the shaft on their first day back on the job.

The air in the shaft was still rank with the odor of the decayed corpses. The miners pressed on, however, blinded by the lure of a paycheck, and began the descent to the bottom of the shaft where Harris had died saving lives.

The first few miners down were stopped in their tracks at the base of the shaft by the sight of a figure looming in the shadows. When the men lifted their carbide lamps to get a better look, they saw the ghostly form of a rotting corpse that they somehow recognized as Harris. The apparition was clinging to the ladder and staring up the shaft at them through empty eye sockets. A whistle cord was knotted around his waist.

Scared out of their minds, the miners scrambled over each other to climb back out of the shaft. In the midst of the mayhem, the whistle that had been disconnected so long ago sounded, its shrill warning rising to such an unnatural pitch that the miners heeded its admonition and never set foot in the mine again.

A terrible mining disaster in 1924 could have been even worse if a heroic miner hadn't sounded his warning whistle; his ghost later sounded the same warning to chase other miners out.

Moose Lake

Moose Lake historian Walt Lower is a veritable fountain of information when it comes to local hauntings and legends. Indeed if it weren't for Walt's careful documentation, the following four stories would likely have been long forgotten.

Here they are in historical sequence, in Walt's words:

Sally Coffee lived south of Moose Lake on Coffee Lake, which was named for her family. She was [a] mother…and was part American Indian.

The best way for the Coffee family to get to Moose Lake was to walk three miles down the [train tracks]. Just before coming to Moose Lake there was a trestle where the [tracks] crossed a river. One day Sally was found dead in the middle of that trestle. She had been shot between the eyes at close range with a large caliber gun. There were powder burns on her face.

This was about 1890 and this much is true. I have talked to people who saw her body [being brought] into town.

The legend is that since her killer was never found she still haunts the trestle. At night the engineer would see a woman standing on the trestle but the train would pass right through her.

The [tracks are] now abandoned so there are no more trains and [there is] no one there to see her.

Lower's next story has to do with the ghost of a man killed in an unfortunate accident while trying to spread some Christmas cheer.

In about 1900 there was a man killed on a road just south of Moose Lake. He worked in Moose Lake and after work he would walk home, which was a ways out of town. Often he would buy a bottle of liquor and drink it while walking. This was a common custom at the time. On the way he would pass a logging crew and he would share some of his bottle with [the crew].

One December evening, when it was getting dark early, he was at the bottom of a hill when a team of horses with a load of logs started coming [towards him]. There were no good brakes on a load of logs like this, so the horses had to run at full gallop down the hill. The walker stood in the middle of the road holding up his bottle to give the teamster a drink. The teamster could not stop and hit the man, killing him.

From that time on no horse would pass that spot without acting up and going out of control. It was as if a spirit affected the horses. It was said that if someone would stop there and take a drink from that spirit, he [would] go away.

Moose Lake has seen its share of tragedies, but none would come back to haunt it like the deadly forest fire of 1918.

On October 13, 1918, a great forest fire swept through the Moose Lake area, taking many lives.

The Lund family had a farm five miles west of Moose Lake. The fire came like a great wave and [they] could see it coming before it arrived. The Lunds were getting ready [to fight] the fire when two of the children, a boy and a girl, bolted and said they were going to Moose Lake [to] get into the [water]. They were never seen again. Their remains were never found. They perished from the fast-moving fire somewhere in the woods.

The Lund family has died out and other people now own the farm. The current owners tell me that they are not alone out there. They feel the presence of other people. At night [they hear] tapping on the windows and someone trying [to open] the locked doors.

The current owners had not heard the story of the lost children when they told me [their story]. Are these children trying to get back home?

Some events in life are just too weird to be chalked up to coincidence. The following story is evidence of that, according to Lower.

I had a friend who I would go target shooting with. He had a rather large collection of different guns, as he had been shooting for a long time.

I also had a collection [of guns], and since we were doing the same sort of shooting, most of the guns we had were the same. [But] there was one gun he had that I did not have.

One day my friend was killed suddenly. His father, who knew nothing about guns, wanted to give me one of the guns. Of all the guns my friend had, his father came over with the one gun that I did not have.

The Ghost of Death

Ghosts are generally thought to walk only at night, but Ardyce Stein, director of the Roseau County Historical Society, may be able to make a case for daytime hauntings with this tale of a *windago*, the Chippewa word for the ghost of death.

The *windago* has been sighted near the Chippewa village at Roseau Lake for years, always in broad daylight on sunny days. Its appearance invariably precedes the death of someone in the village. The Chippewa and Mandan tribes have known the *windago* for so long that there is no oral account of when it first appeared or whom it first marked for death.

Stein says some speculate whether the *windago*, sometimes called fox fire or will-o-wisp, is an apparition or swamp gas. But Jake Nelson and the Chippewa of Roseau Lake swear it is real. Nelson relates three instances of *windago*-related death in the American Indian village in his manuscript "Forty Years in the Roseau Valley."

In the first incident, two of Nelson's young relatives were on their way to school, about a mile west of the village, when they met the ghost on the road. They were quite possibly the first white people to ever see the ghost. They described it as 8 feet tall, dressed all in white, with a large bright star on its forehead. They saw it twice in the same place. Shortly after these appearances, death visited the village. Nelson does not say who died.

The second instance occurred when Nelson's mother and his sister were visiting Anna Mickinock. They were standing in the yard talking about Anna's grandmother, who had been ill for several days, when suddenly Anna pointed south and said, "Grandma die pretty soon, see *windago*." The Nelsons looked where she was pointing and saw a very tall person dressed in white walking across the prairie. It disappeared from sight around a bend and behind some trees. The following day Anna's grandmother died.

Nelson himself saw the ghost the day before the third death. He was in the yard at Mickinock's house when he saw the ghost rise in the south and start walking westward. It stumbled and nearly fell several times, then it ran for about a quarter of a mile. It finally went out of sight behind the east end of the grove on a small ridge. Nelson describes the ghost as being 15 feet tall, dressed in white lace or some similar material and carrying a package in its right hand. Mrs. Mickinock died the next morning.

"The village is gone but is the ghost?" asks Stein. "It appeared again in the early 1930s and created almost as great a reaction as it had [before]. Many people saw it dressed in its flowing white robe and gliding over the reeds of the lakebed."

Stein echoes questions that still are unanswered when he asks, "Was the ghost real or not? Does it ever make an appearance in the Ross area now that the Roseau Lake is drained?"

Fountain of Sorrow

There's an elaborate old fountain in the middle of the Wabasha Street Caves that is said to spray tears of sorrow.

The fountain reportedly came from the garden of a mansion in Minneapolis that was once owned by barbed wire promoter and oilman John Warne (Bet-a-Million) Gates.

Gates went to Texas before the Civil War and later made a fortune selling wire fencing for the Washburn-Moen Company and working in the oil patch. He died in 1911 from a malignant tumor in his throat.

Gates left his fortune to his wife, their son and selected charities. The son, Charlie, reportedly inherited the equivalent of $31 million. Unfortunately, Charlie died two years later from excessive behaviors. His death is said to be responsible for the sorrow emanating from the fountain.

The house in Minneapolis, one of many homes Gates owned across the country, was reportedly torn down in 1933.

Fox Farmer Phantom

The ghost of a fox farmer is said to haunt Lamplighter Park in St. Louis Park. The eerie figure is set aglow by a spectral lantern that lights the path he is doomed to walk for all eternity.

Residents in surrounding neighborhoods have for years claimed to see the ghostly shape at night walking on the other side of the pond. The figure is heading towards the fox sheds that once stood near the water, and it disappears as quickly as it appears.

According to local legend, a small fox fur farm did operate in the area at one time. Red fox fur was all the rage at the time and the farmer raised the animals for their pelts. Neighbors recall seeing the lantern's glow cutting through the darkness of night as the old farmer made his way from the house to the fox sheds to check on his charges.

The fox farmer died an embittered old man, apparently not entirely at peace with the brutal way in which he made a living. Could his midnight sojourns be his way of paying penance to his furry charges?

Kitty Ging

The Bellevue Condominium, formerly the Bellevue Hotel, located at 1229 Hennepin Avenue South in Minneapolis, is home to a trendy coffee shop today, but its past is filled with skullduggery. Indeed some say the ghost of Minneapolis businesswoman Kitty Ging haunts the place, seeking revenge for her cold-blooded murder.

The following article by Joe Zalusky captures the essence of the dastardly deeds that came into play in 1895 in what is arguably the city's most celebrated murder case. Entitled "End of the Rope," the article first appeared in the spring issue of the 1966 edition of the Hennepin History Museum magazine and is reprinted here with permission.

Probably the most noteworthy case in the police annals of Minneapolis was the celebrated "Hayward Case," which involved the crime of murder.

The facts as developed in the trial included the following: Harry Hayward was a young man under 30 years of age, handsome, and holding a fine social position; his father was recognized as a gentleman of wealth and influence in the community.

It seems, however, that young Harry had developed a passion for gambling which he had succeeded in keeping secret from the social world in which he was a favorite.

At that time, in the city, there lived a young businesswoman named Catherine Ging, who did a large, profitable business as a fashionable dressmaker. Both lived in the same apartment building at 1227

Hennepin Avenue, owned by Harry's father. (The building is still standing.)

Unknown to his fashionable friends, young Harry had established a sort of business relationship with Miss Ging and secured her confidence so that she entrusted large sums of money to him.

On the evening of December 3, 1895, Miss Ging rented a team at a local livery stable, located on Grant Street and Nicollet Avenue, and started out alone for a drive.

Some hours later, a chance passerby in one of the suburban districts of the city (Excelsior Boulevard at about 32nd Street) saw a horse apparently running away, and a few rods further discovered the body of a woman lying in the middle of the road, apparently unconscious, and injured in a runaway accident.

An examination showed the woman to be dead, and later the body was identified as that of Miss Ging.

At a postmortem examination it was discovered that the woman came to her death from the wound of a pistol bullet fired into the back of her head by a person or persons unknown.

This was the problem given to police for their solution...but they were up against a stone wall.

After Miss Ging's death, some remarks by Hayward caused rumors to fly indicating that Harry knew more about the murder than he was willing to confess or that anyone had suspected or expected.

William H. Eustis, then the mayor of Minneapolis, together with the whole city detective force under his control, instituted a strict inquiry into all circumstances, and through the well-directed efforts of the

Minneapolis detective force, Harry Hayward was executed a little more than a year later, after one of the most exciting and exhaustive trials known to Minneapolis police history at that time.

It was brought out at the Hayward trial that Miss Ging had, for several months, been advancing him money. He had finally induced her to place a $10,000 insurance policy upon her life, then he persuaded her to take a secret drive with one Claus Blixt, at the end of which Hayward was to meet her to complete some business transaction.

Everything had worked out as planned by Hayward, and Miss Ging was murdered by Blixt. The horse was turned loose to find its way back to the stable. The body tumbled into the road to be looked after by the first chance passerby. Blixt was sent to the state penitentiary where he died many years later. Hayward was hanged a little more than a year after planning and supervising the crime.

The mayor, the detective force and the police were all complimented on the efficient way in which this murder was solved.

Your editor-in-chief had the privilege of seeing the scaffold on which the execution took place the next morning. Contrary to what others might say, the body of Hayward was cremated in Chicago, the ashes returned and laid to rest in the family plot at Layman's Cemetery, Cedar Avenue and Lake Street, Minneapolis.

Ghost Diver

Anyone who has ever gone scuba diving knows the sheer pleasure that comes from viewing the underwater world firsthand. But only a few understand what it's like to have that pleasure turn into terror as it did for the diver in the following story submitted by Mary Hughes of Chicago, Illinois.

When Mary's friend Mark was in his early 20s he worked as a certified diver for the sheriff's department in a small Minnesota town. His job involved diving for the bodies of people who went down in boating accidents.

One day there was an accident on a river. Mark and his colleagues went searching for two men who fell overboard while fishing. The police were parked on a bridge overlooking the river; the divers were in a boat just under the bridge. "They were trained to use the buddy system," Mary says, "and dive in pairs."

Mark went into the water and down about 20 feet and immediately saw the body of one of the men about 15 feet in front of him. He turned back to signal to his buddy, who was facing the other way.

When Mark turned back towards the body, he noticed that it was now closer to him—about seven feet away—and that it was not the body of a man, but the body of a woman with short dark hair and a flapper dress. "Her hands were flowing with the current," Mary says. "She seemed to be beckoning to him."

Mark turned towards his diving buddy again, who signaled that he was going to the surface. Then he turned back towards the woman in the flapper dress to make sure she wasn't a figment of his imagination. He found she was a mere two feet from him—as though she had swum towards him—and she was smiling at him.

"His logical mind told him that this was just a body—maybe the reports were wrong and there were more than two men who had gone overboard," Mary says, "so he reached out his hand and firmly grabbed…the woman's arm. [Then] he shot to the surface, where he found his diving buddy having trouble with his breathing regulator, and his own hand empty."

Mark was embarrassed to mention seeing this woman to his buddy because he felt that she was otherworldly. He told his partner that he was not feeling well and he was going in. His partner was having trouble with his equipment, so they both decided to go up on the bridge for a better view of the search.

Mark's partner was inside the sheriff's van putting his equipment away and Mark was standing on the edge of the bridge looking at the remainder of the search team below when he heard an "*aaahooooogaah*" sound like the horn on an old Model T. He turned towards the sound and saw a Model T driven by the dark-haired woman in the flapper dress cross the bridge in front of him and disappear.

"At this point, Mark became so terrified he ran towards the sheriff's van and asked his partner if he saw the car and the woman," Mary says. "His partner told him that he hadn't seen her, but that the diving crew, as well as others, had seen this woman before.

"Apparently the story goes that she was a mobster's girlfriend who knew too much and was literally given cement shoes and thrown off this bridge in the late 1920s."

The Strange Story of Annie Mary Twente

To be buried alive is a hellish way to die. Without a doubt that was the thought that tortured the grief-stricken parents of young Annie Mary Twente. Other than being obsessed with the notion that the she still lived, what possible reason could they have had to open up the youngster's grave?

The legend of Annie Mary is one of the best-known ghost stories in Minnesota—and with good reason. Records show the six-year-old died on October 26, 1886, of "lung fever." But locals say she suffered a far more gruesome cause of death at the hands of her deranged father, Richard.

Richard Twente was reputed to be a brute of a man whose bizarre behavior struck fear in the hearts of his family and neighbors. Although he was never diagnosed with a mental illness, he was committed to St. Peter State Hospital three times. His genius, witnessed in the single-handed construction of his homestead and granary—the latter considered a marvel in engineering for its time and now listed on the National Register of Historic Places—bordered on madness.

During one of his famous "spells," he reportedly loaded his wife, Lizzie, and his five daughters into a sled in the middle of winter and started across the prairie, running from some invisible threat. It is said he turned back only after his wife begged him to stop, fearing the children would freeze to death in the sub-zero temperatures.

Eventually his strange behavior drove Lizzie to leave him. Or perhaps her departure had more to do with how Annie Mary supposedly died. Legend has it that Annie Mary slipped into a coma after falling from a hayloft. When two days later she still showed no signs of improvement, the little girl's parents gave her up for dead and buried her in the town cemetery.

After Annie Mary's funeral, Lizzie became consumed with an overwhelming sense of dread, perhaps because Richard had not sought a medical opinion before declaring their daughter dead and burying her. Lizzie convinced her husband to open the grave. A most grisly scene greeted them. Scratches from Annie Mary's fingernails were clearly visible inside the coffin as if she had been trying to claw her way out. Her hands, clenched into fists, were holding chunks of her own hair. Her face was frozen in a look of sheer terror.

It is said that Richard, crazed with grief, disinterred his daughter's tiny body and reburied her on a hilltop on the family farm. He then labored like a madman, building a wooden fence around the grave to protect her, from what it is not clear. Later, he replaced that fence with a stone and mortar wall, complete with a locking iron gate, giving the grave site a shrine-like appearance.

Annie Mary's restless spirit reportedly haunted that grave site on the family farm. Her tombstone was said to be cold to the touch in the heat of summer and hot to the touch in the chill of winter. Headlights supposedly failed when drivers neared the location of the grave, and horses reputedly refused to cross the bridge nearby.

Unfortunately, the bizarre legend attracted its fair share of vandals. Donna Weber, news editor of *The Journal, New Ulm*, near Albin Township, where Annie Mary was buried, has followed the legend of Annie Mary's death for years. She detailed the sad state of affairs that willful destruction left the grave site in.

Weber's story "The Legend of Annie Mary Twente," as published in *The Journal, New Ulm* on June 22, 1986. It is reprinted with permission here.

Annie Mary Twente does not rest in peace.

The grave site of Annie Mary Twente in Albin Township near Lake Hanska is littered with broken beer bottles and empty beer cans. Weeds, thistles, prairie grass and volunteer saplings grow within the walls of the 4-foot high, 18-inch fence surrounding the tombstone. The wall is cracked and is covered with moss in some places.

A lone ash tree stands on one side of the entrance to the enclosed graveyard. The charred stump of a second tree is on the other side. Gate hinges project from the wall, but the black iron gate that once swung from those hinges is gone. The gray granite monument stone sits askew on its pedestal. The earth in front of the marker is barren. The stone's inscription [which wrongly records her death as Oct. 28] shows decades of wear, but is clear enough to read:

ANNIE MARY
Born Oct. 14, 1880
Died Oct. 28, 1886
Father and Mother,
May I meet you
in your royal court
on high.
TWENTE

Richard Fischer, owner of the Twente farm in 1986, says that vandals often dug at the grave site. On one occasion, they shoveled two feet down before being scared off. Fischer says the tombstone was stolen too many times to count, and tossed carelessly in a nearby ditch. Even the gate that Richard Twente installed to keep his daughter safe went missing.

Part of Weber's story is about that gate.

As the legend of Annie Mary Twente and the actions of her eccentric father continue to amaze listeners and readers, a foster granddaughter of the Twentes located in Grand Rapids, Minnesota, adds new information about the grave site and the family. "I have the key to the gate," said Elizabeth Thissen. "I found it in my mother's things. It's a flat key and has a cardboard tag reading 'the key to the grave of Annie Twente.'"

She also discovered a poster-size picture of the grave site among her mother's possessions. Thissen's mother was Elizabeth Twente, younger sister of Annie Mary. She married George Groebner, and the family settled elsewhere in Minnesota. Thissen does not remember Richard Twente, but she knew his wife Lizzie, who was her foster grandmother. Lizzie came to live with Thissen's parents because "she couldn't stand to live with (Richard)," Thissen said. According to Thissen, Richard Twente frequently exhibited bizarre behavior. Richard Twente purchased some "worthless land" in Canada and went to live there in about 1920. According to Thissen, he was chopping wood when he suffered a heart attack and died. His body was brought to Minnesota and buried in a Methodist Cemetery next to his wife.

Thissen plans to keep the key to the gate of the grave of Annie Mary Twente.

In 1996, more than 100 years after Annie Mary was first placed in the ground, continuing vandalism at the grave site necessitated the removal of her body for a second time. After negotiating with Fischer for nearly a year, Annie Mary's relatives were finally able to convince him and Albin Township to exhume the little girl's remains and reinter them with her parents' remains in northern Minnesota.

Weber detailed the unearthing of Annie Mary's body in this story, which appeared in the October 18, 1996, edition of *The Journal, New Ulm*.

After Fischer consented to move Annie Mary, her relatives contacted Minnesota Valley Funeral Home in New Ulm about two months ago. The decision to rebury her came at a Twente family reunion. Disinterments usually are not news, said Bruce Savoy, manager of the funeral home. "The stories behind this one makes it unique."

Realizing public knowledge of the disinterment could draw an unwanted crowd, county law enforcement officials were alerted about the plans. No problems developed, and a few neighbors and passersby stopped to ask questions and watch.

With great care, Annie Mary's bones were unearthed. The skeletal remains appeared as they would in a casket today, Savoy said. "Everything was as normal as normal could be for a body buried 110 years ago," Savoy said. "The box was gone...There was no coffin [any]more," Fischer said. Time and the elements

204 Ghost Stories of Minnesota

had claimed the coffin, but its outline was visible, according to Savoy. The body had been placed in the coffin facing east, just as burial practices call for today. "Her hands were crossed," Fischer said.

Brass handles from the coffin and some buttons were found at the site. These objects were placed in the new coffin. The gray granite monument will be restored and placed on Annie Mary's new grave.

About two dozen relatives gathered for the reburial.

The Twente grave site will only live on in memories of people. The stone wall was demolished and removed, and the trees cut down. The land will be returned to crop production—planted, cultivated, harvested. Ironically, Richard built the stone wall to protect the site. But it stood out on the landscape, drawing attention to the plot and contributing to the fascination with the legend. Removing the wall and clearing the site erased the environment that lured people there, an observer said. The desecration and vandalism could not end if the wall remained.

Perhaps, appropriately, the disinterment preceded Halloween, which previously was an impetus for activity at the grave site. "Maybe this Halloween, we can get a little peace," Fischer said.

Ghostly Hitchhiker

Almost every state has a story about a phantom hitchhiker, and Minnesota is no exception. The following tale was submitted by the Ghost Hunters Society of Minnesota and serves as a poignant reminder of why you should never pick up an individual thumbing a ride.

On a cold day in March 2000, a lady was driving along Burnsville Parkway when she saw a male hitchhiker on the road. Normally she wouldn't have stopped—for safety reasons—but on this occasion she did pull over. Later she would say she was not sure why.

The hitchhiker got into the passenger side of the car and the driver started off again. She asked her new companion where he was going but found him to be completely unresponsive. Repeated questioning and other commentary also yielded nothing from the hitchhiker. The driver began to get anxious. She wasn't sure of the fellow's intent.

Then, out of the blue, the man in the passenger seat spoke. He said, "The time is short." The driver looked over in surprise but the man was gone.

Shaken, the woman pulled to the edge of the road and stopped, waiting to regain her calm. Eventually a police car drew up and an officer approached to see if she needed assistance. The driver explained the incident as best she could, not expecting a very enthusiastic response.

She was more than a little surprised when the officer related that five similar episodes had been reported that same month along the same stretch of road.

Ghost Ship

Lake Superior has been the site of many strange and unexplained shipwrecks over the years but none as bizarre as the wreck of the *Bannockburn*, which sank mysteriously on November 22, 1902, with all hands on board.

Barely nine years old at the time of her disappearance, the 245-foot-long *Bannockburn* was a sturdy British-built ship named after the location of the mighty battle of 1314 in which Robert the Bruce won independence for Scotland from the English. Owned by the Montreal Transportation Company, she was one of several British-made steamships on the Great Lakes delivering cargo to American ports such as Duluth. On this November morning, however, she left Port Arthur, Ontario (today Thunder Bay) with a belly full of grain bound for another Canadian port.

The launch was by all accounts uneventful as reported by two passing ships. The first report came from the *Algonquin*, which encountered the *Bannockburn* late in the afternoon near Isle Royal. According to the book *The Great Wrecks of the Great Lake*, James McNaugh, captain of the *Algonquin*, told friends that the *Bannockburn* was in sight when she suddenly vanished without so much as a sound. "McNaugh turned his head away from the *Bannockburn* for a moment," author Frederick Stonehouse writes. "When he looked again, the *Bannockburn* was gone."

Later that evening, the passenger ship *Huronic* also reported sighting the *Bannockburn*, making out her telltale three masts against the backdrop of a brewing winter storm and churning waters. Nothing was thought amiss, however, until the *Bannockburn* was reported overdue that night.

Sightings poured in and were as wild as that evening's winter squall. They placed the ship in a half dozen places at the same time—from running ashore at Michipicoten Island, to crashing on the rocks at Caribou Island, to wrecking near Stannard Rock. Adding to the confusion were reports claiming that relatives of the *Bannockburn* crew were receiving telegrams from their loved ones telling them not to worry and assuring them that the ship was safe and on course.

The winter storm made it impossible to immediately verify any of these wild tales or to launch a search and rescue mission. It was December 1902 before divers took to the icy waters to search for the wreckage of the *Bannockburn*. They came up empty handed. To this day, not a single piece of evidence related to the mighty steamer has ever been recovered.

There are several theories as to what caused the *Bannockburn* to vanish off the face of the earth. Some of the explanations can be traced back to the ancient oral histories of the area's indigenous people. Among the lore of the Chippewa of Lake Superior is the legend of a gigantic sturgeon that could, with the flick of its tail, create a wave so powerful it would turn the mightiest boat into splinters. The phenomenon, called a *seechee* wave, has been blamed for its fair share of wrecks on Lake Superior, but it doesn't come anywhere near to satisfying the curious circumstances surrounding the wreck of the *Bannockburn*.

Another explanation indicts the weather, saying the ship ran afoul in stormy conditions. But this explanation does not clarify how a fully loaded, 245-foot vessel could drop out of sight in a matter of seconds. Nor does it explain how nearly 75 years later, the same eerie circumstances surrounding the disappearance of the *Bannockburn* would again come into play on Lake Superior.

On November 10, 1975, the *Edmund Fitzgerald* sank during a snowstorm with all hands on board. As in the case of the *Bannockburn*, the *Edmund Fitzgerald* was in sight of a nearby freighter, the *Arthur M. Anderson*, moments before it vanished. In addition, that ship's master, Captain Jesse Cooper, had been in radio contact with the *Fitzgerald* master, Captain Ernest McSorley, seconds before the vessel disappeared. The story goes that Cooper lost sight of the *Edmund Fitzgerald* as she headed into a heavy snowstorm, and that the vessel was nowhere to be found when the snow eased minutes later. She had even disappeared from the radar screen of the *Arthur M. Anderson*.

Like the *Bannockburn*, the *Fitzgerald* was reported battling stormy seas near Caribou Island, which lies along the route the vessel took from Port Arthur, Ontario. And therein may lie the key to the mystery.

Recently, marine historians have made a discovery unique to that particular area that just might explain the sudden disappearances of both the *Fitzgerald* and the *Bannockburn*. They have detected a dangerous under-sea rock formation, called a Caribou Shoal, that the ships may have "bottomed out" on. Could it be that both vessels sustained holes and sank out from under their crews before the men realized they were fatally damaged?

Whatever the case, one thing is now certain. The *Bannockburn* has earned the reputation of being the ghost ship of the Great Lakes. The ship's ethereal image is said to be seen frequently at night, steaming across the dark waters where she went down, as if trying to find a safe harbor for her 20 crewmen.

~ The End ~